CHICHESTER

The Chichester Halfpenny was a local token coin minted in 1794 at a time when the city was prospering and was probably at the height of its architectural expression.

Character from that period remains in Chichester still, but without financial aid this unique heritage could be lost.

CHICHESTER
A STUDY IN
CONSERVATION

Report to the Minister of Housing and Local
Government by
G. S. Burrows, MBE, ERD, TD, ARICS, MTPI

London Her Majesty's Stationery Office 1968

Typography by HMSO : J. Saville, MSIA/D. M. Challis

Printed in England for Her Majesty's Stationery Office by
St Clements Fosh & Cross Limited, London

SBN 11 750044 5

Preface

This is one of four reports on the historic towns of Bath, Chester, Chichester and York. They were commissioned jointly by the Minister of Housing and Local Government and the City and County Councils concerned in 1966.

The purpose of the studies has been to discover how to reconcile our old towns with the twentieth century without actually knocking them down. They are a great cultural asset, and, with the growth of tourism, they are increasingly an economic asset as well.

The Civic Amenities Act 1967, sponsored by Mr Duncan Sandys, gave recognition for the first time to the importance of whole groups of architectural or historic value and required local planning authorities to designate 'conservation areas' and to pay special attention to enhancing their character or appearance. While the Act was in preparation, the Government decided that studies should be commissioned to examine how conservation policies might be sensibly implemented in these four historic towns. There were two objectives; to produce solutions for specific local problems, and to learn lessons of general application to all our historic towns.

At the same time my predecessor (Mr Crossman) asked Lord Kennet, the Joint Parliamentary Secretary to the Ministry, to convene a Preservation Policy Group. Its terms of reference are :

(i) To co-ordinate the conservation studies and to consider the results.

(ii) To review experience of action to preserve the character of other historic towns.

(iii) To consider measures adopted in other countries for preserving the character of historic towns and villages, and their effects.

(iv) To consider what changes are desirable in current legal, financial and administrative arrangements for preservation, including the planning and development aspects, and to make recommendations.

Its membership is : J. S. Berry, BSc (Eng), AMICE, MIStructE, MIHE ; H. J. Buck, MTPI, FRICS ; Theo Crosby, ARIBA, FSIA ; A. Dale, FSA ; Prof. Alan Day, BA ; Miss J. Hope-Wallace, CBE ; R. H. McCall ; Prof. N. B. L. Pevsner, CBE, PhD, FSA, Hon FRIBA ; B. D. Ponsford ; H. A. Walton, B Arch, Dip CD (L'pool), ARIBA, MTPI ; S. G. G. Wilkinson (succeeded by V. D. Lipman) ; A. A. Wood, Dipl Arch, Dipl TP, FRIBA, MTPI ; and Lord Kennet as Chairman.

I should like to take this opportunity of thanking very warmly the members of the Group and particularly Lord Kennet. His deep knowledge of historic buildings and enthusiasm for their safety have greatly contributed to the Group's work. This has fallen into two parts.

The first, concluded in the Spring of 1967, consisted of identifying those changes in the law which would improve our national system for the conservation of historic buildings and towns. The views of the Group were taken into account by the Government during the passage of the Civic Amenities Act 1967 and in devising Part V of the Town and Country Planning Bill. The latter provides a much improved system of controlling alteration or demolition of historic buildings, and makes other important amendments to the law.

The second part of the Group's work, that is considering the recommendations of the consultants, begins with the publication of these reports.

The recommendations the consultants make in these reports are numerous and diverse ; with help from the Preservation Policy Group the Government and the local councils concerned will need to consider them carefully. The councils are not committed to adopt any recommendations of specifically local application, nor is the Government committed to adopt the various suggestions of more general application.

We shall now discuss the reports with the councils concerned and with the local authorities of other towns as well. The Preservation Policy Group will co-ordinate these discussions and study their results. Only then will the full value of these reports be seen.

Meanwhile I commend the reports to everyone concerned with the well-being of our old towns, and express the Government's warm thanks to the consultants who produced them.

Minister of Housing and Local Government

Contents

Illustrations

Studies in conservation

Classified guide to selected topics

	Bath	Chester	Chichester	York
Advertisement control				
Areas of special control		L.2.4.14	4.48ff	
			7.64	
			10.03	
Window stickers			7.115	
Agencies for Conservation				
(See also Civic Societies				
Economics & Finance, Ownership)				
Role of the local authority	112	4.3	8.31	6.3
	123	L.3.5.8	8.49	10.3ff
	136		Chapter 9	
	238			
	247			
Historic Buildings Council	112ff	L.4.1	7.139	6.4
Housing Societies		4.3.3		7.37
Land Commission		L.4	8.34	8.13
			Chapter 8	Appendix G
A National Agency?	124-5	4.3.4		10.3
		4.3.5		
		L.3		
University Grants Committee	142			9.20–21
	Appendix B 1a			
Churches				
Condition & Use	62		2.09	6.6
			2.17	8.105
			4.43	8.123
			6.26	
			7.81	
Cathedral cities		3.3	3.03ff	
			3.27	
Civic Societies				
As agents in rehabilitation schemes	100	L.4.6.11	4.44	6.5
			7.138	
			9.08-09	
			9.12	
Conservation Areas				
Conservation section proposed				10.3
Criteria and check list for			Appendix II	
Designation of		4.2	5.01	6.18
Differing views about their proper size and function	35	L.2	5.01-02	10.5
			Chapter 9	10.9
				10.10
Development control in		L.2.4	7.102	10.7
			10.13	
Cost-Benefit Analysis		2.6	8.05-10	Appendix G 4.0
Densities				
Residential		2.7.1	4.02	7.18
			6.76	7.27
			7.33ff	8.12

	Bath	Chester	Chichester	York
Design of buildings				
Control by planning authorities	92ff	2.3		
New design in relation to old buildings	94-100	2.3.9	5.09ff	8.144
	243-5		6.40ff	10.17
			7.66	
			7.99-124	
			9.45ff	
			10.10	
			10.13	
Height of new buildings				8.138
Materials			5.11-12	
			6.40-43	
			7.94ff	
			9.40	
			10.03	
			10.11	
Economics and Finance				
Costs of conversion and renovation	143-4	2.6	Chapter 8	9.15ff
	149-152	4.3	9.49	Appendix G
	156-7	4.4		
	160			
	Appendix B			
Grants				
(a) By local authority	112ff	4.4	4.40	6.15ff
	133	L.4.3	7.139	
	136		Chapter 8	
	161		10.17	
(b) By Exchequer	121ff	4.3	Chapter 8	6.15ff
	239	L.3	10.17	
	241	L.4.1		
Historic Buildings Council and Town Schemes	112ff	L.4.1	7.139	6.4
Housing improvement grants	117ff	L.4.3		
Recoupment			Chapter 8	9.19ff
				Appendix G 5.0
Employment		1.4	3.29-31	3.6
			6.78	3.8
Industry				
Compatibility with historic area	70	2.7.1		3.7
Relocation of		2.7.1	4.02	4.7ff
			4.47	
Legal Aspects				
Present legislation considered adequate	101ff			
	246			
Changes in compulsory purchase and			Chapter 8	
compensation provisions suggested			10.18-19	
Possible conflicts with particular enactments	103ff	2.8.4	7.99	10.7
(e.g. Building Regulations, Housing Acts)	142ff			
General review of legislation		L.1-L.4		
Use Classes Order				8.144
Lists of buildings of special architectural or historic interest				
Assessment of the lists and	18ff	2.8.6	7.130-141	6.11-13
suggestions for revision		L.1	10.12	
Offices	68-69	2.7.4	6.49	3.8
		4.1.3	6.52-54	4.15
			7.65ff	
			7.85	
			10.06	

St. Clements Fosh & Cross Limited, 80/92 Mansell Street, London E1

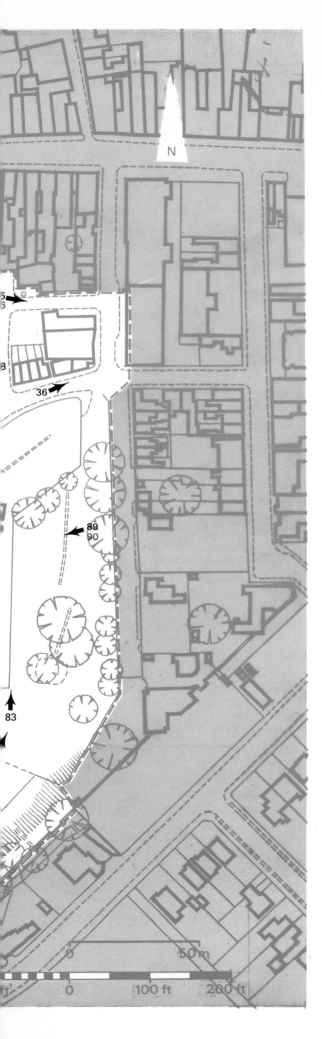

Viewpoints for illustrations

➤   viewpoint

94   existing development (fig no.)

95   recommendations (fig no.)

" . . . . . that precious quality of *character*—a thing that can scarcely be defined but that is most clearly perceptible to all who have sympathy with the history of the place as shown in its architectural expression".

Gertrude Jekyll

This is a report on a study in character conservation of Chichester by Members of the departments of the County Planning Officer, County Architect, County Surveyor and County Valuer of West Sussex County Council and the City Engineer and Surveyor of Chichester City Council under the direction of:

G. S. Burrows, MBE, ERD, TD, ARICS, MTPI
County Planning Officer, West Sussex County Council, in his capacity as Consultant

The study team:
Leader: Miss D. O. Cundall, Dipl Arch, ARIBA

Miss S. Hodson
R. Raynsford
D. P. Thomas, ARICS

Miss B. M. Thompson, BA, AMTPI
J. Vickers, Dipl Arch, ARIBA
K. L. Webb, ARIBA
R. D. Wilson

advised by:

West Sussex County Council
P. W. Bryant, AMTPI
I. Corsie, BSc, AMICE
A. J. Griffin, BA, MCD, ARIBA, AMTPI
R. A. Kennard, Dipl Arch, ARIBA, AMTPI
F. W. Steer, MA, FRSA, FSA Scot, FRHistS
L. A. Tatham, FAI
W. T. G. Wearne, Dipl TP, AMTPI

Chichester City Council
I. Wilson, BSc (Eng), MICE, MIMunE

D. W. Lloyd, BA, AMTPI
assisted the Study Team with the writing and editing of the Report

The views expressed in this report are those of the Consultant and do not necessarily form the policy of the West Sussex County Council or Chichester City Council.

Chichester
September 1967

1 Introduction

1.01   The purpose of this report is to show the way in which the character of a small city of major historical importance and outstanding architectural distinction may be conserved and, to some degree, enhanced, while adapting to the changing needs of the present and future.

1.02   Chichester is a living city, with 20,000 people in its municipal boundaries, and many more in the area around who look to it as a centre for employment, social, welfare and educational facilities, public administration, business activity and transportation. It is in an area growing in popularity for holidays and recreation, and draws to itself an increasing number of visitors on account of its own historical character and visual charm. Any plans for the city must make it convenient and satisfactory for those who live there, work there, make use of the facilities it provides, or visit it for any other reason, and it must take account of changing conditions in the foreseeable future.

1.03   The fabric of a historical city such as Chichester is a record of change, from the days of our earliest recorded history to the present day. The street pattern of the older part of the city is basically Roman and medieval; the buildings are medieval and Georgian, Victorian and modern, the older ones adapted to differing degrees to meet changing requirements and functions through successive ages. The overall pace of change was till recently quite slow; buildings were adapted, occasionally replaced, or newly erected, one by one or in very small groups, even through the nineteenth century (since Chichester was not directly affected by the industrial revolution). It is only recently, with the development of motor traffic, the mechanisation of building techniques, the rapid improvement of living and working standards, and the increasing scale of commercial operations that the rate of change in Chichester (like so many other smaller historical towns) has markedly increased. The safeguarding as a whole, of the historical character of the city, or of a large part of it must therefore be the result of careful and deliberate action.

1.04   It is desirable to preserve the architectural and historical character of a city such as Chichester for two main reasons. Firstly, the environment is extremely pleasant, due to the individual quality of numerous, mostly old, buildings, to the way in which they are grouped, and to the treatment of some of the spaces around them, achieving both harmony and pleasing contrasts in scales, shapes, textures and alignments. Such effects could not be wholly re-created by new development. Secondly, the presence of so many buildings of differing dates, going back in history, imparts a feeling of historical continuity which is becoming more and more valuable in an age in which so much of the environment is contemporary, and indeed often temporary, in character.

1.05   This does not imply that there is no place for new development in an old environment such as that at Chichester; far from it. New buildings may be necessary or desirable, and can be made to fit in with the established environment, and even to enhance it, just as, for instance, Georgian houses fit in so well with medieval buildings. But, because modern building techniques and materials and, in many cases, modern activites carried out inside buildings are so different from those of even the fairly recent past, it requires increasingly greater skill in design for new buildings to fit sympathetically into a predominantly old environment. Aping past styles is becoming increasingly undesirable; new building in old environments should (save in exceptional circumstances) be generally in the idiom of the day and at times of materials for which there is no historical precedent, yet at the same time, fitting satisfyingly and harmoniously into the existing urban context.

1.06 Pressures for change vary greatly, even within the limited central area of a comparatively small town. In some parts mounting commercial turnover and consequent demand for space make it, financially, more and more justifiable for old buildings to be replaced or drastically altered, at least at the ground level. In other parts, existing buildings may prove perfectly adaptable to new uses, or can quite satisfactorily continue in their original use. Elsewhere, buildings (or, often, parts of buildings, such as upper floors where ground floors are fully used) remain empty or under-used and are allowed to deteriorate because of lack of pressure for their suitable use. Preservation problems arise especially in the extreme conditions, when there is too much pressure for change, or not sufficient pressure even to justify, economically, adequate maintenance.

1.07 The most serious disruptive element in almost all old towns is that of motor traffic. All pre-twentieth century development is related to horse or foot transport, and the incursion of motor traffic must result in a change in the character of the environment. Old streets can usually take a certain amount of motor traffic without severe detriment to their character, but in each there is a level of traffic capacity which it is not possible to exceed without serious reduction in the quality of the environment. If the character of historic areas is to be preserved, it becomes more and more necessary to make adequate provision for traffic so that it either avoids them altogether or is reduced to an acceptable amount.

1.08 The recommendations outlined in this report aim to adapt the historical parts of the city of Chichester to fulfil present and foreseeable needs in a way that is economically viable, while preserving as much as possible of their existing and attractive environmental quality, and enhancing them through whatever adaptation and new development are considered desirable and appropriate.

1.09 The overall proposals for the city, including detailed proposals for the central area, are contained in the Reviewed Development Plan, submitted to the Ministry of Housing and Local Government in 1966, which was accompanied by the report entitled *Chichester, Preservation and Progress* (4.02) *. These proposals formed the background for the more detailed study, and subsequent recommendations, made in this Report.

*See bibliography for this publication

2 The city in history

Early history

Roman Chichester

2.01   Chichester was established very soon after the Roman Conquest as the commercial, administrative and route centre of the West Sussex coastal plain, and this remains its basic role today. The first stone defences, enclosing an irregular polygonal area, were built in the late second century and form the basis of the present day city walls, strengthened and heightened in the Middle Ages and restored more recently (fig. 1). There was a gate at each cardinal point, and the cruciform main street pattern established by the Romans is perpetuated to this day.

The Saxon town

2.02   Chichester was one of the 'burhs' fortified by King Alfred in defence against the Danes, and possessed a mint about 930, showing that its military and commercial importance was continued or revived during the Saxon period.

Building of the cathedral

2.03   A minster, dedicated to St. Peter, existed in the city in the tenth century. About 1080 the diocesan centre of Sussex, which had been established by St. Wilfrid near the coast at Selsey about 680, was transferred to Chichester, in accordance with a decree of the Council of London in 1075 that diocesan centres should be in important towns rather than in lesser places. A new cathedral was begun on the site of the Saxon minster under Bishop Luffa after 1091. Building continued through the twelfth century until the consecration in 1184. In 1187 the cathedral was damaged by fire. It was not completely rebuilt, but re-roofed and partly refaced, with a new clerestory and stone vaults, and an entirely new retro-choir which is one of the masterpieces of the architecture of the period. In the thirteenth, fourteenth and fifteenth centuries, alterations and additions were made to the cathedral, the last major additions being in the early fifteenth century, when a spire was added to the thirteenth century central tower (2.22), and the detached bell tower was built.

The cathedral precinct

2.04   Chichester's four main streets divide the city into quadrants. The south-western quadrant became the cathedral precinct, with the Bishop's Palace, the various houses of the ecclesiastical dignatories between the cathedral and the city wall and the College of Vicar's Choral backing on to South Street. Chichester was a secular cathedral served by a Dean and Canons, without an associated monastery such as existed in many other English diocesan centres. In 1205 the bishop

1 *the first stone defences . . . form the basis of the present day city walls* (2.01)

2 *the . . . Cross was built . . . to provide shelter for marketing*
(from a painting by Owen B. Carter showing the top of the Cross as it probably existed in the middle ages) (2.05)

obtained permission from the king to build houses and shops on the strips of land fronting West and South Streets, backing on to the cathedral yard, so shutting off the cathedral from the main streets of the city. The Canon Gate, giving entrance to the southern part of the precinct from South Street, was built in the early sixteenth century.

Markets and shops

2.05   Marketing has always taken place around the meeting of the main streets in the heart of the city and, from the Middle Ages until quite recent times, market stalls extended on certain days along East and North Streets. The very fine octagonal, open-sided Cross was built, not only as an ornamental feature, but also to provide shelter for marketing, by Bishop Story in 1501 (fig. 2). Shops have existed on parts of the frontages to the main streets since the Middle Ages. The annual Sloe Fair established in the twelfth century, an important trading event in the later Middle Ages, is still held, though it has changed its character.

Streets and houses

2.06   In the Middle Ages houses probably lined the four main streets almost continuously, and they often had long rear gardens such as are so characteristic of medieval towns. The rest of the space within the city walls (apart from the cathedral quarter) was only partly developed. The north-west and north-east quadrants had narrow, fairly straight, streets or lanes such as Tower Street, Chapel Street, St. Martin's Lane and Little London, and the wider St. Martin's Square, of which the frontages were partly lined with houses and partly bordered by open land or the grounds of religious establishments. In the south-east quarter is the Pallant, a very distinct enclave, a 'palatinate' which was under the peculiar jurisdiction of the medieval archbishops of Canterbury. It has its own cruciform street pattern (the eastern and western arms of the cross having marked curves), and once had a Market Cross, so forming a sort of miniature town within the city. (The term 'Pallant' is strictly correct, but the four streets are called North Pallant, South Pallant, East Pallant and West Pallant and collectively are generally known today as the 'Pallants'. The area is referred to as the 'Pallants' in the rest of the Report).

Suburbs outside the walls

2.07   Small suburbs developed outside the West Gate, the East Gate (at St. Pancras) and possibly the South Gate at least as early as the thirteenth century. Such suburbs were fairly common outside walled cities; they usually consisted in early times of houses of poorer quality.

The walls, gates and castle

2.08   The Roman city walls were maintained and strengthened, and the Roman city gateways maintained or rebuilt during the Middle Ages. A small castle was established in the north-east quarter of the city in Norman times, but it probably consisted only of a wooden palisade on a motte (of which the motte survives) and a bailey of about five acres, bounded partly by the city wall. The castle was dismantled in 1217.

3 *the Hospital of St. Mary . . . retains the medieval arrangement of living accommodation* (2.10)

Parish churches

2.09 Like many towns of early medieval importance, Chichester had numerous parish churches. There were once ten, all very small, on sites either fronting the main streets (such as St. Olave, North Street), just behind the frontage (St. Andrew, behind East Street), in the subsidiary streets (All Saints-in-the-Pallant), or in the suburbs outside the wall (St. Pancras, and the church of the Holy Sepulchre outside Westgate, the latter now superseded by St. Bartholomew). The important parish of St. Peter-the-Great used the cathedral for parochial services until the present church was built in the nineteenth century (2.22). The only medieval parish churches remaining are St. Olave (recently converted to a religious bookshop) St. Andrew and All Saints-in-the-Pallant.

Other ecclesiastical foundations

2.10 Besides the cathedral and the parish churches, there were three important ecclesiastical institutions. The Franciscan Friary was founded about 1240 and about 1270 occupied the site of the dismantled castle (2.08), where the very fine choir of the friary church (later the Guildhall and now a museum) still stands. The Dominican Friars were established about 1280 in the south-eastern quarter of the city, but nothing of their buildings survive. The Hospital of St. Mary, founded in 1158, moved to its present site near St. Martin's Square about 1290, and its buildings substantially remain. Almost uniquely, the hospital (a home for old people) retains the medieval arrangement of living accommodation in the main hall (or 'nave'), with attached chapel forming a structural 'chancel' to the 'nave', modified by the building of self-contained 'flats' within the hall in the early seventeenth century (fig. 3). The Prebendal School, associated with the cathedral, dates from the early Middle Ages and was refounded by Bishop Story in 1498.

The port

2.11 As well as being a major inland trading centre, with markets and fairs, Chichester was an important port in the Middle Ages. Wool, hides and, later, cloth, were the chief exports, and in the thirteenth century the port was reckoned to be the seventh in England in terms of trade. However, this undoubtedly gives an exaggerated idea of the maritime importance of Chichester itself, since the medieval extent of the legal Customs 'port' is uncertain, and may have varied from time to time. It probably included certain other places on Chichester Harbour and along the Sussex coast. The main landing place for Chichester itself has been, from the Middle Ages, Dell Quay on an arm of Chichester Harbour, about two miles from the city centre. There never seems to have been any substantial number of residential or commercial buildings near the quay itself; the merchants presumably lived in Chichester.

The Reformation and after

2.12 The Reformation did not affect Chichester severely. The two friaries were dissolved, but the cathedral survived, with its endowments and its establishment of dignitaries, and St. Mary's Hospital continued in being. Marketing and port trade continued to flourish. There was one local industry of importance; Chichester became one of the leading needle making centres in the country. Most of the needlers

4 *one of the first important brick houses . . . in West Street* (2.15)

5 *the Market House (by John Nash) was built in 1807* (2.16)

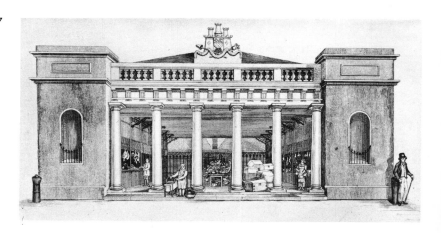

lived in the suburb of St. Pancras outside the wall and worked in their homes or in small workshops. The Cawley almshouse outside the North Gate, of which the original building remains, was founded in 1625.

The Civil War

2.13 The City's loyalties were divided in the Civil War, and it suffered serious damage when it was attacked by the Parliamentarians in 1642. The suburbs outside the walls at St. Pancras and Westgate were badly damaged, and their churches destroyed (2.09). Although the needle industry was revived after the devastation in the St. Pancras area, it never regained its former importance and had died out by the end of the eighteenth century.

The Georgian period

The Golden Age

2.14 The century or so from about 1725 to 1835 was Chichester's 'Golden Age'. Agricultural improvements in the surrounding countryside brought increasing prosperity to the city's corn and stock markets. Businesses serving the agricultural hinterland and the country estates flourished, and much of the local produce was sent coastwise from Dell Quay. The life of the cathedral establishment continued in its placid way, and the Close obtained a predominantly domestic character, since the clergy, after the Reformation, were allowed to marry. Chichester was the main legal and administrative centre of West Sussex, the Quarter Sessions for the division of the county being regularly, though not invariably, held there.

Domestic building

2.15 Until well into the eighteenth century, Chichester's houses were largely timber-framed. Brick was used to a small extent locally in the early seventeenth century, and one of the first important brick houses in the city must have been the house in West Street (originally Westgate House) built by John Edes in 1696 (4.40) (fig. 4). Pallant House was built in 1712 by Henry Peckham, a wine merchant. During the eighteenth century, houses were gradually rebuilt or re-fronted in brick. The four main streets, notably North Street and West Street, retain a large number of substantial town houses of the period. In the Pallants, which became a fashionable residential quarter, most of the houses were rebuilt or re-fronted. Medium sized and smaller houses were built around St. Martin's Square and in the suburbs of Westgate and St. Pancras (which were gradually redeveloped after the devastation in the Civil War), and brick cottages were erected in lesser streets such as Little London and Tower Street. St. John's Street, in the south-eastern quadrant of the city, was developed in later Georgian times. In the cathedral precinct, the Bishop's Palace was greatly altered and the Deanery rebuilt (both about 1725) and other buildings of medieval origin were considerably altered. There was still plenty of space within the walls, much of it occupied by large gardens, including the extensive grounds of detached houses on the fringes of the walled city.

6 *the Providence Chapel . . . built in 1809* (2.17)

7 *elms were planted . . . in 1701* (2.19)

10

Public buildings and institutions

2.16   New public buildings were erected, and old ones improved, during the Georgian period. The Council House, which with its classical facade, projects over the pavement in North Street, dates from 1731 and the adjoining Assembly Rooms (by James Wyatt) from 1783. The Market House (by John Nash) was built in 1807 (fig. 5) (its upper storey was added in 1900). The medieval Market Cross was repaired and the present cupola erected in 1729. The former Corn Exchange, now a cinema with its projecting Doric portico dates from 1832. The Old Theatre in South Street, now an antique market, dates from 1791. The Literary and Philosophical Society was founded in 1831, and later merged with the Mechanics' Institute and occupied a house in South Street, now a club. Some of these institutions illustrate the extent to which Chichester was a minor social and cultural centre in Georgian and early Victorian times.

Churches and chapels

2.17   St. Pancras Church was built in 1750, and St. Bartholomew, Westgate, in 1832, both on the sites of churches destroyed in the Civil War (2.13). Two surviving early Nonconformist chapels are the former Unitarian chapel in Baffin's Lane (now an auction room), built in 1721, and the Providence Chapel in Chapel Street, built in 1809 (fig. 6). St. John's Church was built as an Anglican 'proprietary chapel' in 1823, and retains much of its original internal arrangement. St. Paul's Church, serving the district outside the North Gate (2.25), dates from 1836.

Schools

2.18   The Oliver Whitby School was founded in 1702; it continued till 1950, since which date the endowments have been used for scholarships to Christ's Hospital, Horsham, held by boys from Chichester and certain neighbouring parishes. The Lancastrian School was established in 1811, and was originally conducted on the principles laid down by Joseph Lancaster, a famous educationalist of the time.

The walls and gates

2.19   The crumbling city walls and their surroundings were improved in the early eighteenth century. Elms were planted alongside parts of the walls in 1701 (fig. 7). In 1729 the north and east walls were repaired and the present walks along them constructed, for public use. This was an enlightened way of treating ancient features which was paralleled in both Chester and York at about the same time. Unfortunately, Chichester did not preserve its city gates; the North, South and West Gates were demolished in 1772-3 and the East Gate in 1783.

Transport and trade

2.20   The port prospered; in 1819, 101 ships called there (the highest recorded figure). Most of these sailed coastwise, exporting local produce and probably importing coal and manufactured goods. The opening, in 1817, of the Chichester Canal (a branch of the Portsmouth and Arundel Canal which crossed the plain from Birdham on

8 *there was much space within the city walls in the eighteenth century* (Yeakell and Gardner 1769) (2.25)

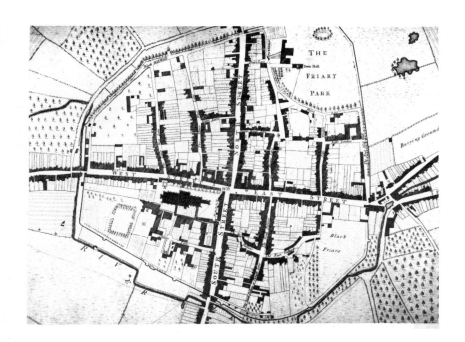

Chichester Harbour to Arundel) and of the Canal Basin in 1822, brought barge traffic right into the city. From 1812 there was at least one coach service to London.

The Victorian period

Commerce and prosperity

2.21 The railway through Chichester was built in 1846, bringing improved communication with Portsmouth, Brighton and (at first indirectly) London. A branch to Midhurst was opened in 1881 and a light railway to Selsey in 1897. Concurrently with the development of the railways, the coastal trade declined. The canal was virtually disused by the end of the nineteenth century, though official closure did not take place till 1928. The city grew very little in population in Victorian times; in 1801 the population was 4,700, in 1851 it was 8,600, and in 1901 it was 8,900. Its importance as a market centre increased; the cattle market became one of the largest in southern England and supplied Portsmouth Dockyard with meat. Certain minor industries, mainly connected with agriculture, and including tanning and brewing, developed. Small and medium sized shops and offices served the surrounding area.

Church restoration and building

2.22 The cathedral, which like most others in the country, had fallen into bad repair by early Victorian times, was restored by stages through the period. In 1861 the central tower and spire collapsed, and were replaced by a replica under the direction of Sir Gilbert Scott (2.03). The fine church of St. Peter-the-Great was built in 1848-52 to the design of R. C. Carpenter, to serve the parish whose congregation had hitherto used the cathedral (2.09). The Methodist Church in Southgate was built in 1876, the Congregational Church, in South Street, in 1892, and a small Roman Catholic Church (recently replaced by a new building elsewhere) in 1855.

Institutions

2.23 Various institutions were established in Chichester during the nineteenth century, partly through the influence of the church and partly because of the city's traditional status as the leading town of West Sussex. The Theological College was opened in 1839, and the Bishop Otter College (for training teachers) in 1850. The Royal West Sussex Hospital (which succeeded the Chichester Dispensary, opened in 1784) was established in 1826, largely through the influence of Dr (later Sir) John Forbes, who was associated with the early development of the stethoscope. The Barracks were built in the early nineteenth century, and later became the depot of the Royal Sussex Regiment.

County administration

2.24 Under the Local Government Act of 1888, the West Sussex County Council was formed, with its headquarters in Chichester. As in other counties, the newly elected Council took over the former administrative functions of the Justices of the Peace at Quarter Sessions, which henceforth became a purely judicial body (2.14).

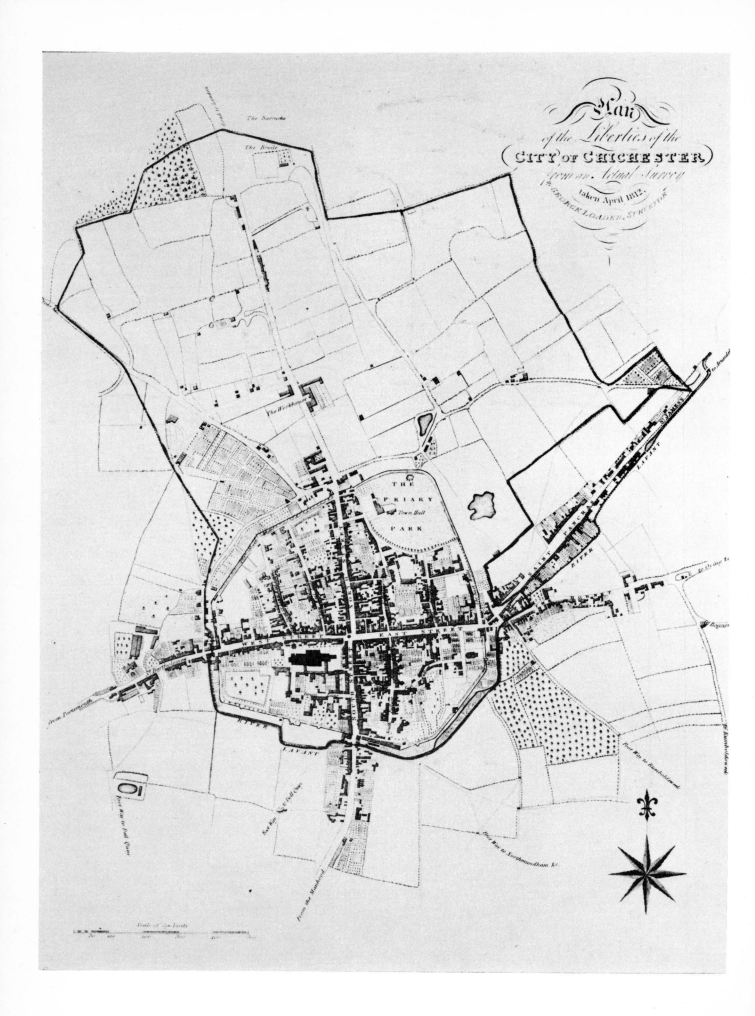

14

9 *development . . . contained within the walls until about 1820* (Loader 1812) (2.25)

Expansion of the city

2.25   There was much space within the city walls in the eighteenth century (fig. 8), and new development was still contained within the walls until about 1820 (fig. 9), apart from the small, old-established 'suburbs' just outside the West, South and East Gates (2.07). Somerstown was an area of close-built streets outside the North Gate, being developed about 1820-40, but has recently been cleared. Small houses, mostly in terraces, were built nearby in Orchard Street (fig. 10) and Franklin Place (following the line of the walls, externally) during the same period. Intermittent, mainly close-built, development began in the Portfield area, to the east of the city, about the middle of the century, and extended southwards and northwards to Whyke and St. Pancras, to form, by the end of the nineteenth century, the most populous part of the city outside the walls (fig. 11). Large houses in extensive gardens began to be built in the later nineteenth century along the Midhurst road at Summersdale, and, to a lesser extent, beyond Westgate towards Fishbourne. There was relatively little development during this period on the southern fringe of the city, which came to be dominated by the railway and the gasworks.

10   *terraces were built nearby in Orchard Street* (2.25)

11 *intermittent, mainly close built development ... to the east ... by the end of the nineteenth century (2.25)*

Changes in the centre

2.26   Physical changes in the central area during the Victorian period were relatively small. The most significant, visually, was the demolition in 1852 of the buildings on the north side of the cathedral, fronting West Street (2.04). This resulted in the cathedral being opened to one of the central streets for the first time since the early Middle Ages. The ground floors of many of the old houses on the four main streets were converted into shops (or if they had been shops already, altered) but the upper storeys usually continued to be used residentially. The scale and resources of most retail businesses during the period did not allow or call for complete rebuilding, but plate glass windows inserted on the ground floor changed the architectural character of the streets (fig. 12). The national banks were established in the city (some of them taking over older local banks) by the beginning of the twentieth century, all in East Street, where the late Victorian Gothic Westminster Bank is a notable landmark. In the lesser streets of the central area there was relatively little change; a few small businesses were established, but most of the Georgian town houses with their large gardens continued to be lived in, while in certain areas there was closer development consisting mainly of cottages. There still remained a good deal of open land, mostly private grounds, within and just outside the walls (6.03). Priory Park, containing the former Franciscan Friary Church (2.10) and the motte of the castle (2.08), and forming the grounds of a private house, was made into a public park in Victorian times.

12 *plate glass windows ... changed the architectural character of the streets (2.26)*

The first half of the twentieth century

Traffic

2.27   The most important factor influencing the life and character of Chichester, like most other towns during the present century, has been the development of motor transport. The city stands at the junction of several roads of national, regional or local significance, carrying both through traffic and traffic bound for the city itself. The resultant congestion in the medieval and Georgian streets of Chichester has, on the whole, probably not been more than usual for a town of its scale and character, but has been accentuated by the peculiar difficulties resulting from the situation of the Cross at the junction of the main thoroughfares.

Road improvements

2.28   The only major road improvement carried out in the area during the first half of the twentieth century was a by-pass, opened just before the Second World War. It took from the city through traffic from west to east as well as much of that to the coast, but still left traffic from the north to the coast to pass through the city. The city centre, especially around the Cross, remained very congested.

Public transport

2.29   By contrast, the principal railway services through Chichester were considerably developed; the main line was electrified in 1938, giving relatively fast and frequent connections with Portsmouth, Brighton and London. The branch line services to Selsey and Midhurst, however, were both withdrawn due to competition from bus services (2.21).

2.30   A network of bus services was developed in the inter-war years, linking Chichester with neighbouring towns and villages.

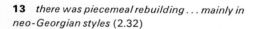

13   *there was piecemeal rebuilding . . . mainly in neo-Georgian styles (2.32)*

Shopping

2.31   Improved transport facilities from the hinterland, parts of which, near the coast, were developed rapidly, strengthened Chichester's importance as a local and minor regional shopping and service centre. At the same time Bognor Regis grew rapidly as a seaside town, with concurrent development of its shopping centre as a rival to that of Chichester, extending its influence over villages to the east and south-east of the city.

2.32   Many of the well known chain and multiple stores moved into Chichester in the inter-war years, and there was piecemeal rebuilding in the central streets, mainly in neo-Georgian styles (fig. 13). New shop fronts and, in places, conspicuous fascias, altered the character of long stretches of the main streets. Fewer and fewer of the upper storeys of the shops continued to be used residentially and were put to storage or other commercial uses, or simply left vacant.

Residential development

2.33   Inter-war suburban development in Chichester was fairly limited, especially compared with that which took place in nearby coastal or near-coastal areas in Sussex and Hampshire. The Victorian residential areas to the east and south-east were extended, and there was some suburban development along the road leading to the south. Since the Second World War, suburban development has been consolidated and in places extended, especially in the hitherto relatively undeveloped area north-west of the city.

Administration

2.34   The widening of the scope of local government, particularly at county level, has been a major element in Chichester's twentieth century development (2.24). County Hall, the neo-Georgian headquarters of the West Sussex County Council, was built in 1936 in the former grounds of a large town house, carefully set and designed so as not to compete with the cathedral in scale of dominance.

Institutions

2.35   Chichester became a major hospital centre with the Royal West Sussex (2.23), Graylingwell and St. Richard's Hospitals, all under the control of the County Council until 1947, when they were transferred to the newly formed Regional Hospital Board.

Industries

2.36   A food processing firm which had been established in the eighteenth century became nationally well known. Existing small industries flourished, and the making of motor vehicle components developed soon after the Second World War.

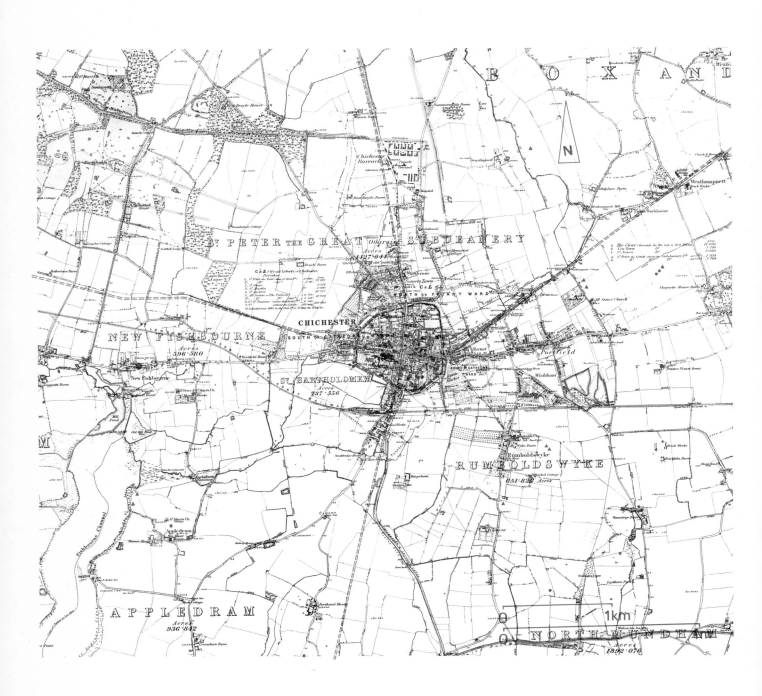

Archaeology

2.37 Archaeological excavations are continually revealing more details of the early history, architecture, social conditions and economic activities of the city and its neighbourhood in early times. The most important are those being carried out at the Roman Palace at Fishbourne on the outskirts of the present city, but many others, collectively having great significance, are taking place both within and outside the city (fig. 14) *.

14 *archaeological excavations . . . are taking place both within and outside the city (2.37)*

- - - - -   Roman wall

.ᐱ.   pre Roman finds

⊤   pre Roman earthworks

.·.   Roman finds

- - -⧓- - -   Roman roads

.·.   post Roman finds

*See bibliography for archaeological report

15 *from afar the cathedral spire dominates the area* (3.03)

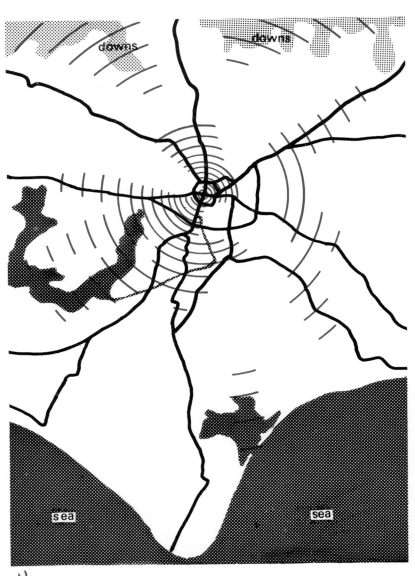

))) areas from which the cathedral is visible

3 The city today

3.01   This chapter attempts to portray the character of the city as it is today. The first section deals with the city's physical characteristics, the second (3.15) with its social and economic functions.

Physical characteristics

The setting of the city

3.02   Chichester lies on the coastal plain between the South Downs and the sea. The Downs begin about three miles north of the city; the nearest part of the open coast is at Bognor Regis about seven miles to the south-east. To the south-west is Chichester Harbour with its many dividing channels, one of which is about two miles from the city centre at Dell Quay and Fishbourne. The city stands between two large urban concentrations, that centred on Portsmouth and Southampton to the west, and that centred on Brighton and Worthing to the east. Portsmouth is 18 miles, and Brighton 32 miles away.

The cathedral

3.03   From afar the cathedral spire dominates the area between the sea and the Downs (fig. 15), rising above the flat, hedged fields when seen from the coastal plain, or pointing from a hazy landscape when viewed from the Downs (fig. 17). The city is still small and compact enough for the cathedral, with its surrounding roofs, to appear in effective contrast to the adjoining countryside when it is seen from higher ground or approached over the level coastal plain.

3.04   Nearer at hand, the best general views of the cathedral are from the south-west; from a train approaching from Portsmouth, or from Westgate Fields (fig. 18), where the spire, the western towers, the Bell Tower and the upper parts of the main structure can be seen rising behind the city wall, which here has no buildings outside it and which, in its moderate height, gives scale to the great building behind.

3.05   Within the city itself, the spire is only sometimes dominant, because buildings often hide it completely, even in the central streets. This, however, accentuates the effect when it suddenly does come into view, as from West Pallant, the middle part of East Street, the Friary Lane area, Tower Street, County Hall forecourt, or from many places around St. Martin's Square. From the walk along the North Walls, the whole length of the cathedral can be seen rearing magnificently above the lower buildings.

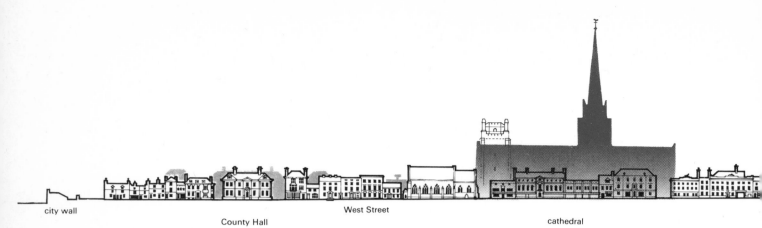

city wall   County Hall   West Street   cathedral

16 *the predominant scale is that of three domestic storeys . . . County Hall is the largest secular building, but does not reduce the dominance of the cathedral (3.09)*

17 *the cathedral spire . . . pointing from a hazy landscape when viewed from the Downs (3.03)*

Cross   East Street   city wall

18 *the best general views of the cathedral are . . . .*
from Westgate Fields (3.04)

20 *the skyline of Chichester . . . contains nothing which competes . . . with the cathedral (3.09)*

21 *brick and tiles of a rich red hue were the predominant local materials . . . stucco was first used locally about 1820 (3.10)*

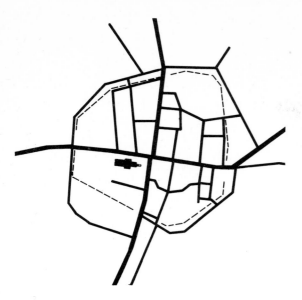

19 *the historical core of the city . . . the form of an irregular polygon (3.06)*

Form of the city

3.06   The city wall defines the historical core of the city, and encloses an area in the form of an irregular polygon about half a mile across (2.01) (fig. 19). At the centre of the city is the medieval Cross (2.05), from which the four main streets run towards the cardinal points, North Street being offset slightly to the east. At the end of these streets were the four city gateways; although they were all demolished in the eighteenth century (2.19) their siting is still apparent. The main streets, except for parts of West Street, are almost entirely given over to shopping.

3.07   The four quadrants of the city have varied and intricate patterns of streets, mostly narrow. Both the north-east and the south-east quadrants have large numbers of Georgian houses, many still residential, others used as offices, and considerable open areas adjacent to the wall. The south-west quadrant contains the cathedral and its precinct (2.04), and the north-west quadrant is mostly occupied by County Hall (2.34) and recent residential development.

3.08   The pre-Victorian city extended a little beyond the city gateways, and these areas immediately outside the wall are mixed in character, with old and new commercial and residential buildings.

Scale of buildings

3.09.   The skyline of Chichester, on its flat site, is full of minor variations, but contains nothing which competes in dominance with the cathedral when the city is seen from far (fig. 20). Within the city, there is a great variety of architectural scale. In the main streets building heights vary, but within a fairly narrow range; the predominant scale is that of three domestic storeys. In the lesser streets there is a greater range of scales. County Hall is the largest secular building, but does not reduce the dominance of the cathedral (2.34) (fig. 16).

Building materials

3.10   The cathedral and a few other important medieval buildings are of light grey limestone, from Caen and the Isle of Wight. Most houses before the middle of the seventeenth century were timber-framed, and although few street facades now display this method of construction, it is still evident in the back elevations and interiors of buildings which have been later re-fronted (2.15). During the eighteenth century, brick and tiles of a rich red hue were the predominant local materials, occasionally mixed with blue-grey brick. Stucco was first used locally about 1820 (fig. 21). Flint was used for some buildings in the Middle Ages (such as the small parish churches) and for many small buildings and boundary walls (usually bonded with brick) in the eighteenth and nineteenth centuries. Occasionally it is found, to good effect, on the facades of important Georgian houses. The city thus shows a great variety of building materials, but the predominant ones are the grey stones of the cathedral and the red brick of the Georgian facades, the other materials providing interesting variants which, in the older buildings, are harmonious. The effect has, however, been considerably weakened in the shopping streets by the recent introduction of unsympathetic materials on some shop fronts and facades.

22 *large gardens . . . pleasantly walled . . . containing
mature trees* (3.11)

23 *well wooded grounds . . . into which the recent
buildings* (of the Theological College) *. . . fit admirably*
(3.12)

Open spaces

3.11 Not all the inner city is closely built. There are still some large gardens to houses, often pleasantly walled in old brick or flint, and containing mature trees which are so often effective incidental features of the street scenes (2.15) (fig. 22). Even where large gardens or grounds to former houses have been partly built over, or put to other uses, something of their old quality has often been retained with the preservation of trees and boundary walls, as around County Hall and in some of the central car parks. The only large public open space within the city centre is Priory Park, set against the city wall in the north-east quadrant (2.26).

3.12 Although development extends beyond the city wall in nearly every direction, there are still places where open land adjoins or comes close to the outside of the wall. Westgate Fields, partly used as school playing fields, and partly public open space, extend right up to the wall on the south-west side of the city (3.04). They have recently been planted in specific places with trees, and they merge visually with the well wooded grounds of the adjoining Theological College, into which the recent buildings designed by Ahrends, Burton and Koralek fit admirably (fig. 23). On the north-eastern side, Jubilee Park, a small open space planted in Victorian times, makes a fine foreground to the city wall. Oaklands Park stretches from just outside the site of the North Gate for some distance northwards, and provides a setting for the Festival Theatre (3.33).

The suburbs

3.13 The suburban districts of Chichester extend, in most directions, roughly from half to three-quarters of a mile from the city wall. The highest overall density of residential development is to the east and south-east. On the northern and western fringes, lower density housing, much interspersed with trees, prevails, and to the north the grounds of the hospital and barracks, as well as Oaklands Park, form considerable breaks in the continuity of development. As the city is approached from several directions, particularly from the west, north and north-east, the suburbs are hardly apparent and there is a quick transition from the open country into the heart of the city.

Location of industry

3.14 Industry (3.31) is mainly concentrated in the two industrial estates established since the Second World War on the southern and south-eastern fringes of the city, but some old established industrial units are scattered elsewhere in the city. The only one of considerable size within the walls is a food processing factory (2.36), partly in a late Victorian building and partly in recent extensions, in the north-east quadrant.

F

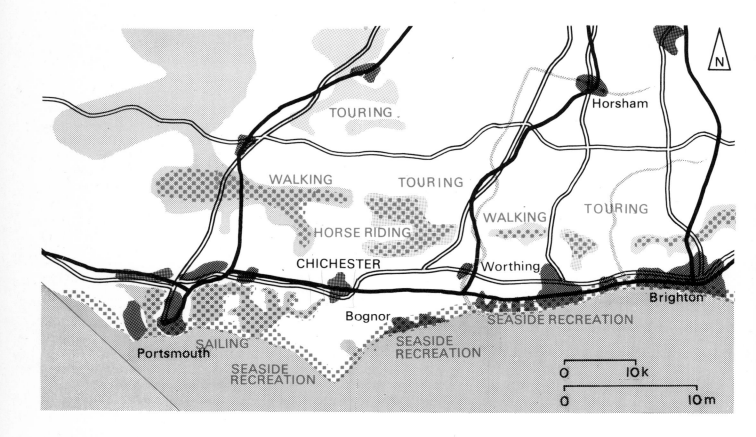

Social and economic functions

The city in the region

3.15   Chichester is the dominant urban centre for a large area of the coastal plain and South Downs (3.02).

3.16   The A27 trunk road, which runs from west to east across southern England, by-passes the city on the south side. Several other roads of regional or local significance, many of them taking considerable traffic in the holiday season, converge on the city (2.27).

3.17   The electrified railway from Portsmouth to Brighton passes through Chichester. East of the city it connects with a line to London via Horsham. Through most of the day trains run hourly to London (taking 100 minutes), twice hourly to Brighton and three times hourly to Portsmouth.

3.18   Chichester is also the centre for a network of local bus routes, extending as far as Brighton, Horsham, Midhurst, Petersfield and Portsmouth.

3.19   Chichester's area of dominant influence as a shopping centre includes the Selsey peninsula with its seaside villages (3.24), the yachting villages on the harbour, a large part of the mainly agricultural area of the coastal plain and an extensive, though thinly populated, area of the South Downs further north. This area of dominant influence is limited to the south-east by competition from the shopping centre at Bognor Regis (2.31). Westwards the strong pull of Portsmouth and its satellite centre of Havant become apparent towards the Hampshire border, but northwards and north-eastwards there are no comparable centres for a very long way. This catchment area had a resident population of about 51,000 in 1961 (including the city itself), which is steadily increasing. In the holiday season the figure is considerably higher.

3.20   Larger regional centres such as Portsmouth and Brighton (3.02) draw specialised trade from the Chichester area.

3.21   Many of the larger villages in the city's area of dominance have an increasing number of local shops, and so are becoming less dependent on Chichester for their more basic needs.

3.22   For other services, entertainment or cultural facilities provided in the city, the catchment area depends on the circumstances of each particular facility and the location of comparable or better facilities of the same sort in neighbouring places.

3.23   The city and its surroundings are a favoured residential area for retired people, and for people employed in neighbouring larger centres or even, to some extent, in London. An increasing number of people maintain accommodation near the harbour or coast, or in the surrounding countryside, as well as in London.

3.24   The area around Chichester, with its beaches, harbour and downland is becoming increasingly popular for outdoor recreation (3.02) (fig. 24). Bognor Regis is a very well known holiday resort. Selsey and East and West Wittering (in Chichester's area of influence) are large and fast growing seaside villages.

25 *Chichester Harbour is one of the most popular yachting centres* (3.25)

3.25 Chichester Harbour is one of the most popular yachting centres in southern England, and was designated as an Area of Outstanding Natural Beauty in 1964 (fig. 25). The recently opened yacht basin at Birdham supplements the long-established facilities for yachtsmen at Bosham, West Itchenor, Dell Quay and other villages bordering the harbour.

3.26 The nearby South Downs are within an area designated as an Area of Outstanding Natural Beauty in 1966.

The Cathedral

3.27 It is as a cathedral city that Chichester is primarily known (3.03). The direct influence of the cathedral on the life of the city is difficult to evaluate. Congregations at the main services are, by present day standards, large. Visitors are numerous, and the cathedral draws people to the city on its own account. The presence of the cathedral clergy and choristers and the special atmosphere of the Close add intangibly to the character of the whole city. The cathedral chapter has gained a reputation as a patron of arts; the painting by Graham Sutherland and the reredos by John Piper have attracted national attention. The Southern Cathedrals Festival, an annual event in which the choirs of Chichester, Salisbury and Winchester take part, has been held since 1960, alternately in each of the three cathedrals.

3.28 The Prebendal School, a preparatory boarding school which has the choir boys among its pupils (2.10), and the Theological College, training priests for the Church of England (2.23), are institutions associated with the Cathedral.

Shopping

3.29 Chichester is a flourishing shopping centre with branches of many of the well-known multiple stores, chain stores and super-markets, one sizeable department store and some specialised establishments, such as antique shops and shops catering for the needs of yachtsmen (3.19). Over 1,600 people are employed in retail trades in the city.

Offices

3.30 Chichester is a very important administrative centre. The West Sussex County Council, with its headquarters in the city (2.34), administers an area with a population of about 450,000; the Chichester Rural District, with its council offices in the city, has a population of about 58,000; the city itself has a population of about 20,000. Chichester is also a centre for local offices of ministries and other national government organisations. There are professional and commercial offices serving the district and also administrative offices of national or regional business concerns, some of them recently established. Altogether over 3,800 are employed in offices in the city, almost half of them in local government or crown offices.

Industry

3.31 Though not primarily an industrial centre, Chichester has a number of medium sized to small industries (3.14).The largest, and one of the oldest established, is a nationally known food products firm. Other firms are engaged in the making of component parts for vehicles, the supply and manufacture of agricultural requirements, and the processing of dairy products. Over 2,700 people are employed in industry in the city and its immediate vicinity.

Institutions

3.32 Chichester has a number of institutions of regional or wider significance (2.23). There are three hospitals, the Royal West Sussex Hospital, Graylingwell Hospital and St. Richard's Hospital. The depot and training centre of the Royal Military Police has been recently established at the Barracks. The Bishop Otter College is a Teacher Training College with about 600 students and is extending. The Theological College has about 55 students. The College of Further Education, established in 1964, offers full and part-time courses on a wide variety of subjects, serving an area including Bognor Regis, Arundel, Petworth and Midhurst as well as Chichester. It had 577 full-time and 5107 part-time students in the summer of 1967. Extensions to the College are being carried out.

Cultural and recreational facilities

3.33 The Chichester Festival was inaugurated in 1962 with the opening of the Festival Theatre, designed by Powell and Moya to an unusual plan with an open stage. The Festival extends over the summer months, and in its first five years has established a national reputation.

3.34   The Theatre, when not required in connection with the Festival, is used occasionally for other dramatic or musical productions. The eighteenth century Assembly Rooms (2.16) are also available for public gatherings.

3.35   Of three cinemas which existed ten years ago, only one is now open (2.16).

3.36   The Museum, opened in 1964 in a converted grain store in Little London, has a small but well arranged local collection. The former Franciscan Friary Church in Priory Park contains Roman and other antiquities, but is open to the public only one day a week. St. Mary's Hospital, which is the city's most important historical building after the cathedral (2.10), is regularly open to visitors. The recently excavated Roman Palace at Fishbourne, within the city boundaries, will soon be open as a major historical attraction (2.37).

3.37   The city has fairly wide facilities for outdoor recreation in the various public open spaces, notably Priory Park (fig. 26) and Oaklands Park (3.11). One of the former gravel workings on the eastern and south-eastern outskirts of the city is used for boating. Others are, or will be, used for fishing, and almost all offer habitats for wild life, attracting many naturalists. The nearest facilities for yachting and the harbour itself are at Dell Quay (3.25). A swimming pool, opened in 1967, is in one of the former cinemas (3.35).

Traffic

3.38   Traffic has increased at an unforeseen and unprecedented rate almost everywhere in the country since the 1950s. This fact has been more generally appreciated since the publication of the Report *Traffic in Towns** which emphasizes the likely continuation of a high rate of increase during the next fifty years.

3.39   Traffic conditions have steadily worsened in Chichester, causing congestion in the central streets, particularly in the four main streets around the Cross (2.27), with the usual consequences of deterioration in conditions for the pedestrian and steady debasement of the quality of the environment.

3.40   Westgate Fields Road, opened in 1965, has taken some traffic off the central streets, but its true value as a traffic route will not be realised until the rest of the future ring road system, of which this forms a part, has been completed (4.09).

*Traffic in Towns, a study of the long term problems of traffic in urban areas; reports of the Steering Group and Working Group appointed by the Minister of Transport. The Working Group was headed by Colin Buchanan, BSc, MTPI AMICE, ARIBA (now Professor Buchanan)

the Review of the Development Plan was sub-mitted to the Minister in 1966 (diagrammatic) (4.02)

0   1 km.

0   1 mile

4 Preservation and progress

The approved Development Plan

4.01   The original Development Plan for Chichester, prepared under the Town and Country Planning Act, 1947, was submitted to the Minister of Housing and Local Government in 1952 and was approved in 1958, and remains the statutory plan.

The reviewed Development Plan

4.02   The Review of the Development Plan was submitted to the Minister in 1966 (fig. 27) together with a Town Centre Map, at a larger scale (fig. 28), and the report *Chichester Preservation and Progress* * explaining the proposals in detail as supporting documents. This awaits his decision. It provides for development in the city and the immediately adjacent rural areas up to 1981 and, within the city centre, includes development likely to take place up to 1986. Provision is made for an increase in the population of the city and its immediate environs from 22,300 in 1961 to about 31,000 in 1981. Several areas, mainly in the outer parts of the city, are allocated for new housing development. Social and educational needs are provided for in appropriate places. Additional land is allocated for industry adjoining the two established industrial estates, mainly to accommodate existing industries which are unsuitably sited elsewhere in the area. In particular, provision is made for expected future volumes of traffic in a way which causes as little detriment as possible to the city as a whole.

4.03   The proposals for the central area aim primarily at retaining and enhancing the city's special architectural and historical character while catering for the future needs of the population. This will be broadly achieved by: (1) preserving buildings with architectural and historic value, and ensuring that new buildings and the treatment of the spaces around them are harmonious; (2) re-designing the pattern of traffic circulation, including the means of servicing commercial premises and the provision of car parking facilities, so that traffic is wholly excluded from parts of the principal streets (except for emergency traffic) and reduced to acceptable limits in others; (3) making provision for increased shopping and commercial facilities, and some new residential accommodation, mainly in certain relatively small areas of development.

4.04   The reviewed Development Plan also identifies certain areas of distinctive environmental quality (fig. 29) to which reference is made in Chapter 5 (5.15).

trunk roads

primary roads

public car parks

shopping

business

residential

places of assembly

civic and special uses

hospitals

schools and colleges

industry

cattle market

open space

*See bibliography for this publication

37

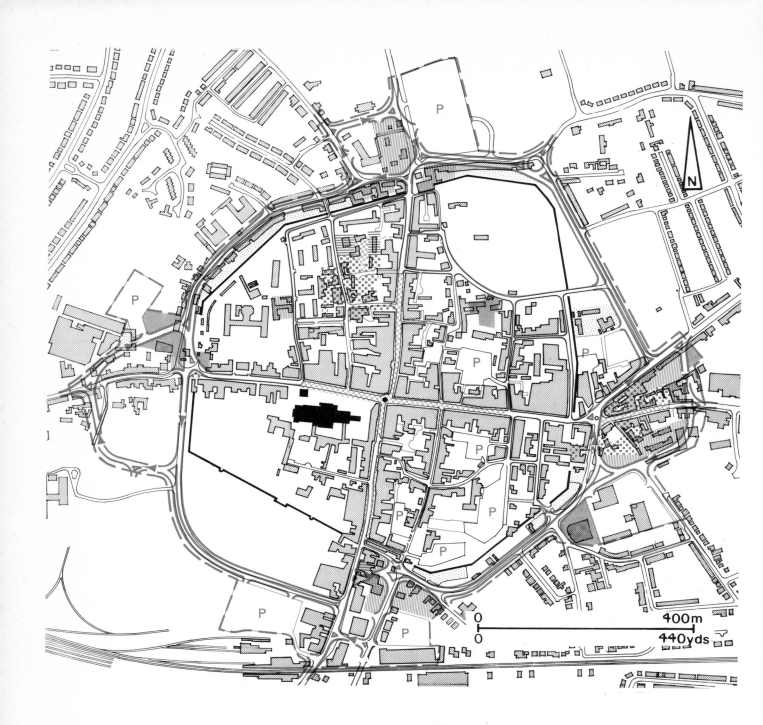

central area boundary

primary roads

distributor roads

service roads and areas

P   public car parks

traffic-free areas

open spaces

shopping

business

residential

civic, cultural and special

Traffic

4.05 The rapid and continuing rate of increase in vehicles on the roads (3.38) is even more marked in South-East England than in the country as a whole.

4.06 In 1962 the figure for car ownership in West Sussex was 0.17 cars per head, as against 0.13 nationally. It has been calculated that car ownership in West Sussex will have increased to 0.41 cars per head of population in 1981. Taking other factors also into account, it is estimated that the amount of traffic on the local roads in 1981 will be 2.7 times greater than in 1962.

4.07 Major road proposals are made to cater for through traffic and local traffic and, in particular, to re-route most of the traffic now passing through or penetrating the central area (3.39) (fig. 30).

Through traffic and approaching traffic
4.08 A line for a new length of trunk road to the north of the existing A.27 trunk road between Chichester and Havant has been proposed for construction at some time in the future. It will link, at a proposed multi-level junction at Fishbourne, with the west end of the existing Chichester by-pass, with the present trunk road, and with Fishbourne Road (which leads into the city centre). From the junction a new road is proposed which will connect with the existing Selsey and Wittering roads south of the city. This new road will be designed to take the greater part of the traffic coming from the Selsey peninsula, which will then enter the city from the west instead of, as it does at present, over the level-crossing on the south side of the city. At a later stage, after 1981, another new road is proposed running northwards from the Fishbourne road junction along the line of the present Midhurst branch railway, to link with the Midhurst road north of the city, so providing the much needed north-south by-pass.

Ring road and circulatory system
4.09 The existing ring of roads encircling the walled city will be greatly improved. Orchard Street, Franklin Place, New Park Road and Market Avenue will be widened and formed into dual carriageways.

4.10 Improved connections between the existing roads and the ring system will be made outside the sites of the four former city gates (3.06). Conventional intersections, such as roundabouts, at these points would use a large amount of land, and would result in the destruction of much property with serious detriment to the visual character of these parts of the city. Therefore, one-way circulatory systems have been devised, partly along stretches of existing streets and partly along new roadways to be constructed. These will enclose comparatively large areas, where some existing development will be retained, and where provision will be made for fairly substantial new development.

4.11 Until the new western by-pass has been built (4.08), through traffic from north to south will use the ring road system.

Traffic in the City centre
4.12 Connections with the central street system will be made at the circulatory systems outside the sites of the city gateways, and at Chapel Street, Priory Road and St. John's Street.

4.13 As much traffic as possible will be excluded from the city centre, within the walls and the ring road. It will be virtually limited to cars going to and from the minor car parks, vehicles servicing shops and business establishments, vehicles connected with residential

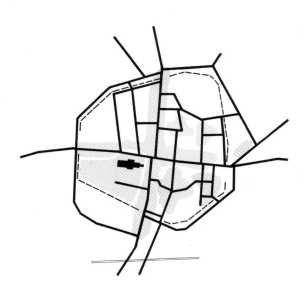

29 *areas of distinctive environmental qualities* (4.04)

30 *major road proposals . . . to re-route most of the traffic now passing through . . . the central area (4.07)*

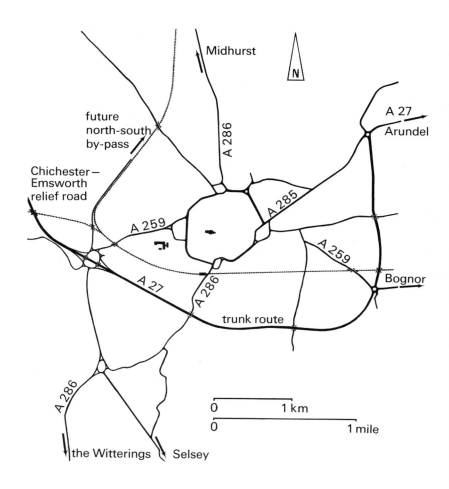

properties and places of public assembly within the central area, and the proposed passenger transport service (4.31).

4.14   It is intended that a central pedestrian precinct shall be formed by closing the four main streets to vehicular traffic for varying distances from the Cross; West Street as far as Tower Street; North Street up to Crane Street; and East Street to Little London. South Street will be closed for a short distance to just north of Cooper Street (a small cul-de-sac on the eastern side), but beyond that will be kept open for use only for servicing traffic. Nearly all the other existing streets in the city centre will remain open, some as distributor roads, bringing essential traffic to the city centre, and the others as service roads, taking traffic from the distributor roads into servicing areas, car parks or individual properties. Most will be one-way streets. In this way, a network of thoroughfares will be available for the essential traffic which cannot be excluded from the city centre. Most of these streets are narrow, some curve and many have considerable environmental quality, but the estimated amount of traffic that would use them will not be sufficient to cause serious detriment to their quality. It must be emphasised that the Minister's decision on the Reviewed Development Plan has not been reached and that until this has been done the proposals in the original Statutory Development Plan (4.01) remain operative.

Servicing of shops and business premises
4.15   A survey was made in January 1965 of shop servicing in the central area, which established the proportions of deliveries in heavier and lighter vehicles, the frequency of deliveries and the times when most deliveries took place.

4.16   Because the four main streets will be largely closed to traffic, alternative arrangements are proposed for servicing many of the premises fronting these streets. This can be achieved from existing roads, from existing or proposed car parks or from stretches of new service roads which will be constructed. The proposed pattern for servicing has been devised so that there is a minimum of detriment to the attractive character of some of the existing streets. It would be impossible to provide alternative facilities for servicing the premises on the west side of South Street without grave detriment to the character of the cathedral precinct, and it is mainly for that reason that South Street will remain open for servicing vehicles up to a point about 100 yards south of the Cross. It is possible that new methods of wholesaling and retailing may change the pattern of servicing, and therefore the proposals are flexible.

Car parking
4.17   Surveys were carried out in September 1964 to establish the number of cars parked in the city and the average durations of stay in different types of car park. Taking future trends into account, it is estimated that about 7,000 public car parking spaces will be needed by 1981.

4.18   The number of parked vehicles which can be accommodated within the walled city is limited by the restricted capacity of the local roads and the undesirability, for aesthetic reasons, of building high multi-storey car parks within the walls. Existing car parks in the central area will be retained with some minor extensions, and are intended mainly to accommodate vehicles parked for relatively short periods. Most of the future car parking provision will be made outside the city walls on sites of large capacity, all easily accessible from the ring road or the circulatory systems (4.09), and connected with the city centre by pedestrian ways crossing over or under the main traffic routes.

The provision outside the walls will include some three- or four-storey car parks. There is also provision for some private car parking in the city centre in connection with business and office establishments.

Land and building uses

4.19   The Reviewed Development Plan does not propose any major changes in the established land and building use pattern in the centre of the city, except in the fairly limited areas where redevelopment is proposed. The established shopping area along the four main streets will remain at approximately its present extent, although small scale rebuilding and better use of existing premises may intensify the degree of activity within the present shopping area. Certain areas, including the Pallants and the County Hall area, are allocated primarily for office purposes. Fairly substantial areas in each of the four quadrants are allocated primarily for residential purposes. These predominant uses do not necessarily preclude other uses compatible with the character of the areas.

Areas of redevelopment
4.20   There are four main areas of redevelopment proposed in the Reviewed Development Plan, at Chapel Street, and outside the sites of the East, South and North Gates.

4.21   The Chapel Street area (around the junction with Crane Street) contains a number of old and obsolete properties of little or no architectural or historical value. The area will be redeveloped mainly as a small shopping precinct, forming an extension of the established shopping area in North Street, and including a health centre. This development is programmed to take place in the early stages of the plan (7.144).

4.22   The redevelopment area outside the site of the East Gate will be contained within the proposed traffic circulatory system, and will be centred on The Hornet. Not all the property in this area is likely to be rebuilt; it is intended that certain buildings which are of architectural merit, or are substantially built, will be incorporated within the redeveloped area. This redevelopment, which makes provision for new shops and offices, is mainly programmed to take place after 1981 (7.144).

4.23   Redevelopment on parts of the east frontage of Southgate and around the north end of Basin Road will be mainly for office and other business uses. This is programmed for the early part of the planning period, in conjunction with the new link road from Market Avenue to Southgate which will form part of the traffic circulatory system at the southern entrance to the central area (4.10). Redevelopment of part of the area outside the site of the North Gate, within the proposed traffic circulatory system, has already taken place, and the remainder is programmed for a fairly early stage in the planning period (7.144).

4.24   There is likely to be a continuing increase in shopping turnover in Chichester, for several reasons. The population of the area in which Chichester is the dominant shopping centre is likely to rise from about 51,000 in 1961 to 74,000 in 1981 (3.19). At the same time, there will probably be a general increase in the amount of money which each person spends in a year. Expenditure by holiday makers in the area will also increase. It is likely, however, that there will be improved shopping facilities for local needs in the larger villages within Chichester's area of dominant influence, slightly reducing their dependence on Chichester as a shopping centre (3.29).

New shopping provision

4.25 Much of the additional shopping expenditure is likely to occur in the established shopping centre, either by extension of premises, or more intensive use of existing buildings.

4.26 The Reviewed Development Plan makes provision for 106,000 square feet of new shopping floor space in the city centre (including provision for the replacement of premises disturbed by redevelopment). Some of this new shopping space will be in the Chapel Street area (4.21), soon to be redeveloped. The rest of the proposed new shopping provision will be in The Hornet area, where redevelopment is programmed to take place in over fifteen years' time (4.22).

4.27 Changes in shopping habits, national or local, which are now unforeseen, may result in the future need for additional shopping provision in the city being greater or less than that now envisaged. The extent of the shopping floor space to be provided in The Hornet might, therefore, in the light of changing circumstances, be either increased or reduced before detailed plans for the redevelopment of the area are drawn up.

Office development

4.28 Provision is made for some new office development. Much of the new development for offices and other business purposes will take place in the redevelopment areas at Northgate, The Hornet and Southgate.

Programming

4.29 The proposed development in the City Centre is programmed to be carried out in fourteen stages up to 1986 (7.144).

Studies undertaken since the submission of the reviewed Development Plan

Mini-bus feasibility study*

4.30 Most of the existing bus routes in the city take in two of the main shopping streets and pass the Cross, the vehicles in some cases turning there with difficulty and requiring police assistance to go against the stream of traffic (fig. 31). If buses were retained in the city centre after the formation of the pedestrian precinct around the Cross (4.14), they would have to be diverted through the narrow minor streets, which would be impracticable and very destructive of the quality of the environment.

4.31 It is therefore proposed that, with the exclusion of traffic from the future pedestrian precinct, buses will come no nearer to the centre of the city than the ring road (4.09). Distances from future bus stops to the centre of the proposed precinct would be about 500 yards. The possibility of operating a mini-bus service between points outside the city centre (adjoining the main bus stops and the outer car parks) and the proposed pedestrian precinct has been investigated with regard to general feasibility and cost. A number of alternative routes

*See bibliography for mini-bus feasibility study

31 *bus routes . . . requiring police assistance to go against the stream of traffic* (4.30)

32 *the mini-bus would be an . . . electric vehicle* (4.32)

for mini-buses in the city centre has been suggested. It is considered that such a scheme would be of particular value to elderly people and for shoppers with heavy loads.

4.32 The mini-bus would be an eight- to ten-seater battery electric vehicle (fig. 32). Greatly improved vehicles of this type are being produced, and it is likely that they will make an important contribution to public transport requirements in town centres in the near future. Mini-buses would not disrupt the environment by reason of noise or fumes, and would be easy to manoeuvre in narrow streets. Research on this subject indicates that a mini-bus service is feasible, although no details have yet been decided.

Bicycles *

4.33 Bicycles are popular in Chichester, probably mainly because of the flat terrain. At busy times they are parked in a continuous line against kerbstones, mainly in North and East Streets near to the Cross. The survey of cyclists and bicycle parking revealed that shopping trips by cyclists are regular and frequent. It is estimated that there is a need for accommodation to park from 60 to 70 bicycles in or near the central shopping area.

Pedestrian movements *

4.34 In November and December, 1966, an interview survey of pedestrians in the main shopping streets was carried out, in order to establish the pattern of use they made of these streets. This revealed a complicated system of individual movements, including the frequent retracing of steps over the same lengths of street. Many short cuts off the main streets, especially between shops and car parks, and also through certain shops, are well used. The mean average distance walked by pedestrians in the city centre is 0.6 miles, and the majority (77%) walk between a quarter of a mile and one mile. It was noticeable that elderly people frequently make quite lengthy journeys on foot. The survey has reinforced the emphasis placed by Professor Buchanan in *Traffic in Towns* (3.38), on the importance of walking in town centres, and the need to give urgent consideration to the safety, comfort and convenience of pedestrians in the central area.

Visual survey

4.35 A comprehensive visual survey of street scenes in the city centre was undertaken in order to facilitate the choice of a section of the city for special study (5.29) (fig. 33). Field sketches recorded the detailed elements of the changing scenes (fig. 34).

*See bibliography for bicycle and pedestrian surveys

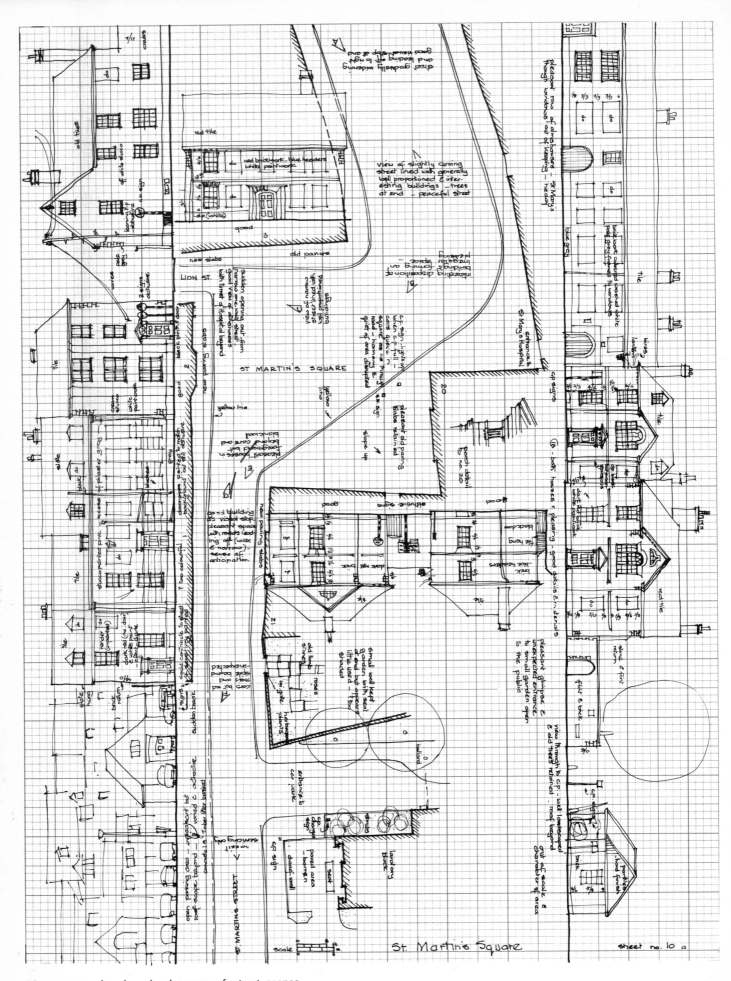

33 a comprehensive visual survey of street scenes
in the city centre (4.35)

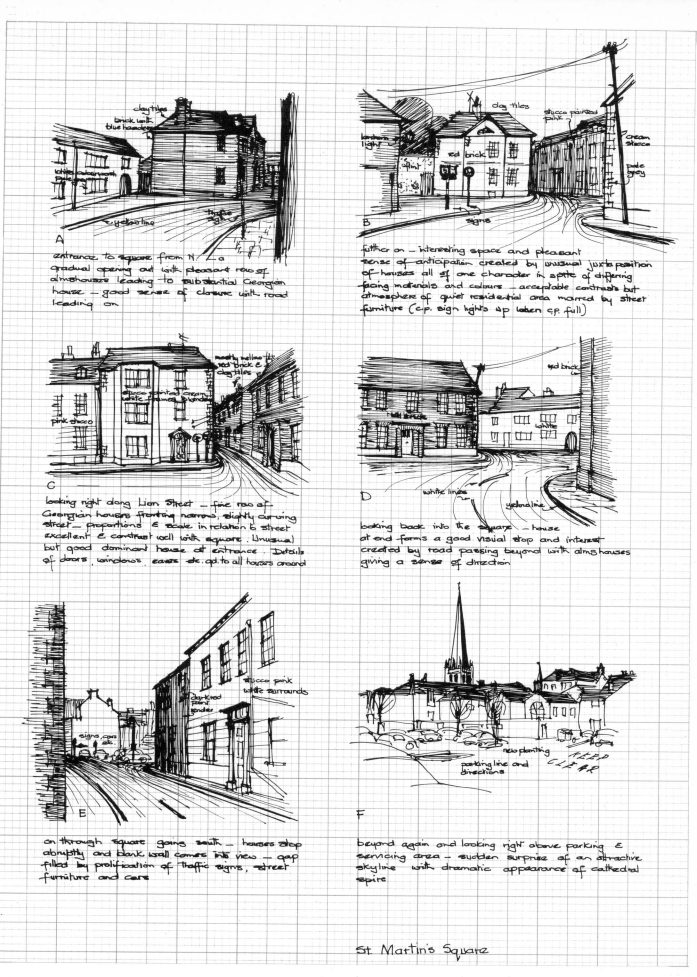

A

entrance to square from N. a
gradual opening out with pleasant row of
almshouses leading to substantial Georgian
house — good sense of closure with road
leading on

B

further on — interesting space and pleasant
sense of anticipation created by unusual juxtaposition
of houses all of one character in spite of differing
facing materials and colours — acceptable contrasts but
atmosphere of quiet residential area marred by street
furniture (cp. sign lights up when cp. full)

C

looking right along Lion Street — fine row of
Georgian houses fronting narrow, slightly curving
street — proportions & scale in relation to street
excellent & contrast well with square. Unusual
but good dominant house at entrance. Details
of doors, windows, eaves etc. apt to all houses around

D

looking back into the square — house
at end forms a good visual stop and interest
created by road passing beyond with almshouses
giving a sense of direction

E

on through square going south — houses stop
abruptly and blank wall comes into view — gap
filled by prolification of traffic signs, street
furniture and cars

F

beyond again and looking right above parking &
servicing area — sudden surprise of an attractive
skyline with dramatic appearance of cathedral
spire

St. Martin's Square

34 *field sketches recorded the detailed element of the
changing scenes (4.35)*

Future development in the wider regional setting

South Hampshire Study

4.36   In the *South Hampshire Study*, a report on the feasibility of major urban growth in the Southampton-Portsmouth region prepared by Colin Buchanan & Partners in 1966*, a possible pattern of very large-scale urban development was suggested, mainly in the form of an urban 'corridor' extending from north of Southampton to Havant and Emsworth, about 10 miles west of Chichester. Development in this form could result in the addition of a population of about a million, by the end of the century, to the present total of over 770,000 in the Southampton-Portsmouth region. No decision has yet been reached on the possibility of development on such a scale or in this particular form, but any major increase of population and commercial development in South Hampshire would have important effects on Chichester and its surroundings, particularly regarding the use of the locality for recreation, and as a 'dormitory' for the developing region.

4.37   The *South Hampshire Study* also examines the possibilities of further development outwards from the Southampton-Portsmouth region in the fairly distant future, if and when most of the suitable and available building land within the region is taken up. One possibility suggested is that of an eastward extension of the 'corridor' of development through Chichester to link with the existing built-up area along the south coast around Brighton and Worthing. This would completely change the character of Chichester, making it a part of a much larger urban environment, rather than a small self-contained city in a predominantly rural area.

Preservation and improvement

Listed buildings

4.38   Chichester has 243 buildings of architectural or historical interest on the statutory list prepared under the Town and Country Planning Acts, and 266 on the supplementary list. 208 of those on the statutory list and 179 of those on the supplementary list are in the central area. These are large numbers for a city of Chichester's size, and the length of the list emphasises the city's historical interest and architectural quality. However, 29 buildings formerly on the statutory list (6 in the central area) and 120 on the supplementary list (51 in the central area) have been demolished since 1950 (fig. 35).

4.39   The extent of the loss of listed buildings in Chichester in recent years is a reflection of the seriousness of the problems of preserving distinctive old buildings, especially in intensively commercialised areas. These problems have tended to increase during the last decade or so, through a number of causes, some of which are readily apparent, and which are analysed in greater detail in later chapters of this report. Commercial, especially retail, units have tended to become, on the average, larger, and less readily accommodated in old buildings of small scale and often of irregular form. Chain stores, multiple stores

---

**South Hampshire Study:* Report on the feasibility of Major Urban Growth (Colin Buchanan and Partners, in association with Economic Consultants Limited), published by HMSO 1966

and, in recent times, supermarkets have become important features in shopping centres such as Chichester. These types of shop usually require fairly extensive purpose-built or easily adaptable premises often with wide street frontages. Costs of repair work to old buildings have greatly increased, and with intermittent periods of economic stringency money has not always been readily available for maintenance and repair work when it has been most needed. Traffic requirements have resulted in the demolition of some listed buildings on the edges of the central area, particularly in the vicinity of the junctions of the new Westgate Fields Road (3.40) with Westgate and Southgate.

Achievements in preservation

4.40 Under the Local Authorities (Historic Buildings) Act, 1962, Local Authorities are empowered to make contributions towards the repair and maintenance of buildings of historic interest. The West Sussex County Council makes grants under this Act, and £5,000 was set aside for this purpose, for the first time, in the County's Annual Estimate for 1967-68. These grants are for essential repair and maintenance work on historic buildings on the statutory list. As a general rule, those which are considered to be of importance to the County as a whole, and not to a particular town or village, are given preference. However, response from owners of historic buildings has so far been disappointingly slow, relatively few applications for grants having been received at the time of writing this report. This may have been due to lack of publicity for the grants scheme. The City Council has not so far made any grants under the Act.

4.41 However, much that is positive has been done in recent years to preserve in good order the buildings which form important parts of the city's architectural heritage. The City Council has undertaken the repair, at considerable expense, of the city walls, the Cross, the former Franciscan Friary church, and other notable buildings. A very large number of fine buildings in the city centre in both commercial and residential use have been sympathetically restored and maintained by private owners or occupiers. The conversion of the main part of the former Corn Exchange into a cinema in the inter-war years (2.16) and, much more recently, of the rear part into offices (fig. 36), and the alteration of a former grain store in Little London into a museum (3.36) are notable examples of adaptations to new uses of buildings, of which the distinctive external quality has been retained or enhanced. Another example of a good conversion is the building commonly known as Wren House (formerly Westgate House), but now to be known as John Edes House (2.15). This was until lately the County Library, and is now being converted by the County Council into the County Records Office.

4.42 Many of the Georgian or earlier houses in the central area are still in residential use and are maintained in good order, especially in and around the Pallants, St. Martin's Square, Little London and Westgate. The relatively high prices which some of these houses obtain on the property market indicate the extent of the demand for 'period' houses in the city centre.

35 *buildings of architectural or historical interest . . .*
(some of which) *. . . have been demolished since 1950*
(4.38) (1910 base map)

Keep
(Site of)

rs' Monastery
(Site of)

179
9·548

RY PARK

178
2·317

M.48·2 Pavilion

180
·780

Re

B.M.45·8

44

46

B R O A D

47

Friends' Meeting
House
Fn.

206a
329·936

Band Stand
B.M.49·7

CH

LITTEN TERRAC

45

JUBILEE PARK

NEW CITY WALL

NEW CITY PARK ROAD

EAST ROW

B.M.48·9

School

48

School

Grave
206
1·01

Ch.

B.M.50·5

EASTGATE SQUARE

Golf Club
(Site of)

Fire Eng.
Station
B.M.49·1

P.H.

P.H.

45

Chapel

W.M.

Chapel

Corn
Exchange

NEW TOWN

Chap.

Tower

ST. JOHN'S STREET

MARKET ROAD

Rectory

Lavatory

43

B.M.44·9

CATTLE M

207

43 Urinal

231
·391

Tower

B.M.43·9

Allotment Gardens
232
3·103

CALEDON

CLYDESDALE AVENUE

STIRLING ROAD

238
5·383

ursery

	buildings on statutory list
	buildings on supplementary list
	buildings on statutory list demolished and not replaced
	buildings on statutory list replaced
	buildings on supplementary list demolished and not replaced
	buildings on supplementary list replaced
	other buildings demolished
	new buildings

36 *the conversion of . . . part of the former Corn Exchange into . . . offices . . . of which the . . . quality has been retained* (4.41)

37 *car parks have a pleasant quality* (4.46)

Ecclesiastical buildings

4.43   Many of the historical properties in the city are owned by the Church. The cathedral's endowments are partly used for the maintenance of the buildings in the precinct, the vast burden of maintaining the cathedral itself being borne largely through voluntary contributions. Of the small old city churches (2.09) a few are still in regular use, but one (St. Andrew's) is in poor repair. The conversion of the former St. Olave's into a religious bookshop is a notably successful example of a suitable use being found for a former church building.

The urban scene

4.44   Greater emphasis has been made in recent years in the safeguarding of improvement of groups of buildings, which need not necessarily all be remarkable individually, but which compose attractive townscapes. An important step was taken in 1962 when the City Council, advised by the Civic Trust, initiated a scheme of improvement for the whole of North Street with Sir Hugh Casson as consultant. This included the redecoration of premises in an harmonious way and, in some cases, the improvement of the detailed treatment of the shop frontages. The Market House (2.16) was restored. The Chichester Civic Society was instrumental in carrying the scheme into effect.

4.45   Redevelopment has been carried out piecemeal over the years in the central shopping streets. In the past it has often been in neo-Georgian style. Recently, however, the County and City Councils have pursued a policy requiring new building in the central streets to be harmonious in scale and materials, and encouraging development in the modern idiom. The building designed by Sir Hugh Casson, at the corner of North Street and East Street, has set a high standard in these respects.

Tree preservation and planting

4.46   The City Council has a policy of conserving good trees and planting new ones. This is particularly apparent in the car parks which have been formed in the last few years, largely in the former grounds and gardens of town houses (3.11). Many of the fine old trees have been preserved, as well as stretches of boundary walls, and new trees have been planted. As a result, many of the car parks have a pleasant quality, unusual for this type of environment (fig. 37).

Reducing the impact of major development

4.47   Two gasholders are conspicuous landmarks in the southern part of the city centre (2.25). The Southern Gas Board intended to replace these with a single larger gasholder. Agreement was, however, reached with the County Council and City Council that the new gasholder should be sited on the Industrial Estate, and that storage should be at high pressure, so enabling it to be much smaller than was originally intended, and less intrusive visually than the existing gasholders. The County and City Councils will pay part of the cost of the new equipment in order to cover the extra expenditure. Eventually, the existing gasholders will be removed. This is a notable example of satisfactory agreement between local authorities and statutory undertakers, leading to reduction in the detrimental visual impact of necessary development.

38 *advertising* 1956 (4.49)

39 *advertising in the city centre* . . . (now in an) . . .
Area of Special Control 1967 (4.49)

Control of advertising

4.48   The City Council has, for several years, pursued a rigorous policy of advertisement control. As a result, unacceptable advertisements have been removed from the main streets and hoardings eliminated in the city centre (except in the vicinity of the railway station).

4.49   Advertising in the city centre is controlled by the County of West Sussex (Area of Special Control) Order, 1965, made under the Advertisement Regulations, 1960. It was confirmed by the Minister of Housing and Local Government, and came into operation in March, 1967 (figs. 38 and 39). The area to which the Order relates includes most of the rural parts of West Sussex, together with the centre of Chichester and small parts of two other towns. Such Areas of Special Control have been defined elsewhere in the country, but outside West Sussex they are either entirely rural or include only small parts of towns of exceptional character, such as the immediate surroundings of cathedrals. Chichester is the only place where an entire town centre, including an extensive commercial area, is included within an Area of Special Control.

4.50   The effect of the Order generally is to prohibit certain kinds of advertising altogether, notably commercial advertising which is unrelated to the land or buildings on which it is displayed, and to impose on other forms of outdoor advertising restrictions more severe than those applicable under ordinary planning control.

5 Conservation and environment

Central Chichester as a conservation area

5.01   The area to which this Report refers is what may broadly be called the central area of Chichester. The central area of any town is the focus of the commercial, administrative and cultural activities of the town and its dependent hinterland. Usually, where the town has grown gradually over a long period, the central area is the oldest part of the town, containing all or most of its notable historic buildings, and such is the case in Chichester. The central area of Chichester comprises the original city, bounded by the Roman and medieval wall, together with additional areas immediately outside the sites of the four main gates, into which the development spread from an early date, and over which present day central uses have extended. The whole of this central area is considered as a Conservation Area (fig. 40).

5.02   The Memorandum on Conservation Areas relating to the Civic Amenities Act* contains the following passage:

Clearly there can be no standard specification for conservation areas. The statutory definition is 'areas of special architectural or historic interest the character or appearance of which it is desirable to preserve or enhance', and these will naturally be of many different kinds. They may be large or small, from whole town centres to squares, terraces and smaller groups of buildings. They will often be centered on listed buildings, but not always; pleasant groups of other buildings, open spaces, trees, an historical street pattern, a village green, or features of archaeological interest, may also contribute to the special character of an area. It is the character of areas, rather than individual buildings, that Section 1 of the Act seeks to preserve. Conservation areas will, however, be numerous; they will be found in almost every town and in many villages. It is for this reason that the Act requires all Local Planning Authorities to designate them. The Ministers hope that they will take early steps to establish areas. They suggest that they should do so one by one, starting with the areas in which conservation measures are most urgently needed, because of pressure for redevelopment or because of neglect and deterioration, instead of waiting until they are ready to move on a broad front. The need is very urgent in many historic towns.

Environment

5.03   The term 'environment' is now frequently used in planning contexts, but with varying and sometimes imprecise connotation. Literally the word means simply 'surroundings'. In the report *Traffic in Towns* (3.38), the term is used in relation to general comfort, convenience and aesthetic quality of the physical surroundings for living. In this report the word is used for the somewhat wider connotation, relating to the quality of the surroundings within which

*Joint Circular from the Ministry of Housing and Local Government and the Welsh Office (Ministry of Housing and Local Government Circular 53/67), Civic Amenities Act, 1967—Parts I and II, 7th August 1967

most urban activities take place. An area with a distinctive recognisable character is defined as an environmental area (5.15).

5.04   The proper study of urban environment should take account of numerous factors which may be defined under three broad criteria (5.27):
(a) Uses and activities
(b) Conditions which affect people's well-being, convenience and safety
(c) Visual considerations

Uses and activities

5.05   In any Town Centre there is an immense variety of uses to which land and buildings are put, and activities carried on in them. However, there are areas where certain activities dominate, such as those connected with shops, offices, a major institution, or even particular types of shop or office. Such dominance of certain activities (but not necessarily to the exclusion of others) gives special character to the environment of particular parts of towns, and gives rise to planning problems which may be quite distinct from those which arise in neighbouring areas where different activities predominate.

Conditions affecting well-being, convenience and safety

5.06   Professor Buchanan has emphasised in *Traffic in Towns* how the quality of urban environment generally is deteriorating with the increasing intrusion of motor vehicles. Deterioration in terms of safety is obvious and measurable, through mounting accident statistics; deterioration in terms of what may broadly be called convenience and well-being is less tangible and, in many respects, not susceptible to precise measurement.

5.07   Increased danger from motor vehicles leads to increased anxiety on the part of pedestrians and, perhaps still more, on the part of those who are concerned with the safety of dependants or relatives, particularly children. More vehicles mean more noise, more vibration and more atmospheric pollution, with effects that are obviously unpleasant, detrimental to the comfort of people in the vicinity, and probably harmful to their health.

5.08   A good environment should be convenient to the people who live, work and move in it. The degree of convenience depends upon the planning of the buildings and spaces in relation to each other and to those in adjoining areas; the disposition of the uses to which they are put; the means of pedestrian movement affecting the area in question; the connections with points at which vehicles (private or public) may be left or entered; and to the extent to which there is any conflict between pedestrian movement and the passage of vehicles.

Visual considerations

5.09   In Britain, historic towns have usually been developed piecemeal. Even where a new town was founded with a regular plan, or a Roman plan was inherited (as at Chichester), the buildings were generally erected one by one, or in very small groups at a time. It was not until the eighteenth century (except in London), that the development of whole streets or squares to pre-determined designs became at all common, and then mainly in major cities or resorts. In smaller towns such as Chichester the process of piecemeal small-scale replacement and accretion has continued, each new piece of development being fitted into an already existing environment.

5.10   Old towns were filthy by modern standards, were inconvenient in very many ways, were disease-ridden and, in parts, poverty stricken. Progress in material standards has eliminated or reduced the filth, the diseases and the poverty; former hovels have disappeared, leaving mainly the more substantial buildings to survive until the present day. Because of these material improvements, historic urban environments, when well conserved, can now be appreciated to a degree which would have been unimaginable in historic times.

5.11   However, with improved living conditions, there has been a general decline in the collective appearance of towns. Reasons for this are many and complex, and cannot all be analysed in a short space. One very important factor has been the enormously enlarged scope of building materials available. Until the early nineteenth century, the range of materials in any locality was fairly limited; in Chichester it included limestone, flint, timber, brick (nearly all in a consistently rich red), clay tiles and plaster or stucco (3.10). This range was sufficient to give interesting visual variety. Structurally, such traditional materials had considerable limitations. Openings in walls were necessarily restricted in width, and windows had to be subdivided into small panes. The scale of the exteriors of buildings was usually set by that of the repeated small openings, with their predominantly vertical emphasis. Because of the restrictions of colour and texture range, and limitations of scale, imposed by the available materials, old towns tended inevitably to attain a consistent character.

5.12   With the present almost unlimited range of materials available, it has become necessary to exercise very great care and discretion in the selection of materials and in the determination of the scale and proportion of new buildings in old environments. Unless this is done, the old consistency of external appearance and proportions, established through the limitations of the old materials, is reduced or lost.

5.13   Even in Chichester, with its predominantly attractive character, parts of the environment are visually unsatisfactory, or lacking in coherence. Here (as is made apparent in the survey and analysis of the Study Area, Chapter 6) there is need for improvement and re-creation of the quality of the environment.

5.14   The form and appearance of spaces around and between buildings in towns are as important as those of the buildings themselves. Urban spaces have often undergone considerable change. Where they were once paved or roughly finished they are now covered with tarmacadam. Even where grass and plants now grow there has often been great change; for instance the ground around the cathedral, which was formerly a graveyard, now has only a few tombstones set in a large expanse of close mown grass. An extreme example of change in the relationship of buildings to each other and to spaces is afforded by the setting of the cathedral. Originally it was hemmed in to the north as well as to the east by buildings which fronted the neighbouring streets; but the demolition of the houses to the north in 1852 (2.26) created a space of entirely new dimensions, so that the cathedral and buildings on the north side of West Street came to be seen in a new relationship to each other and to the rest of the inner city.

new
residential
area

County Hall
precinct

Westgate

West Street

cathedral precinct

Westgate Fields

main shopping street

main shopping street

St. Martin's
Square

Little London

main shopping street

the Pallants

St. John's

Priory Park

Jubilee
Park

N

P

P

P

P

P

P

P

P

P

P

0

0

400m

440yds

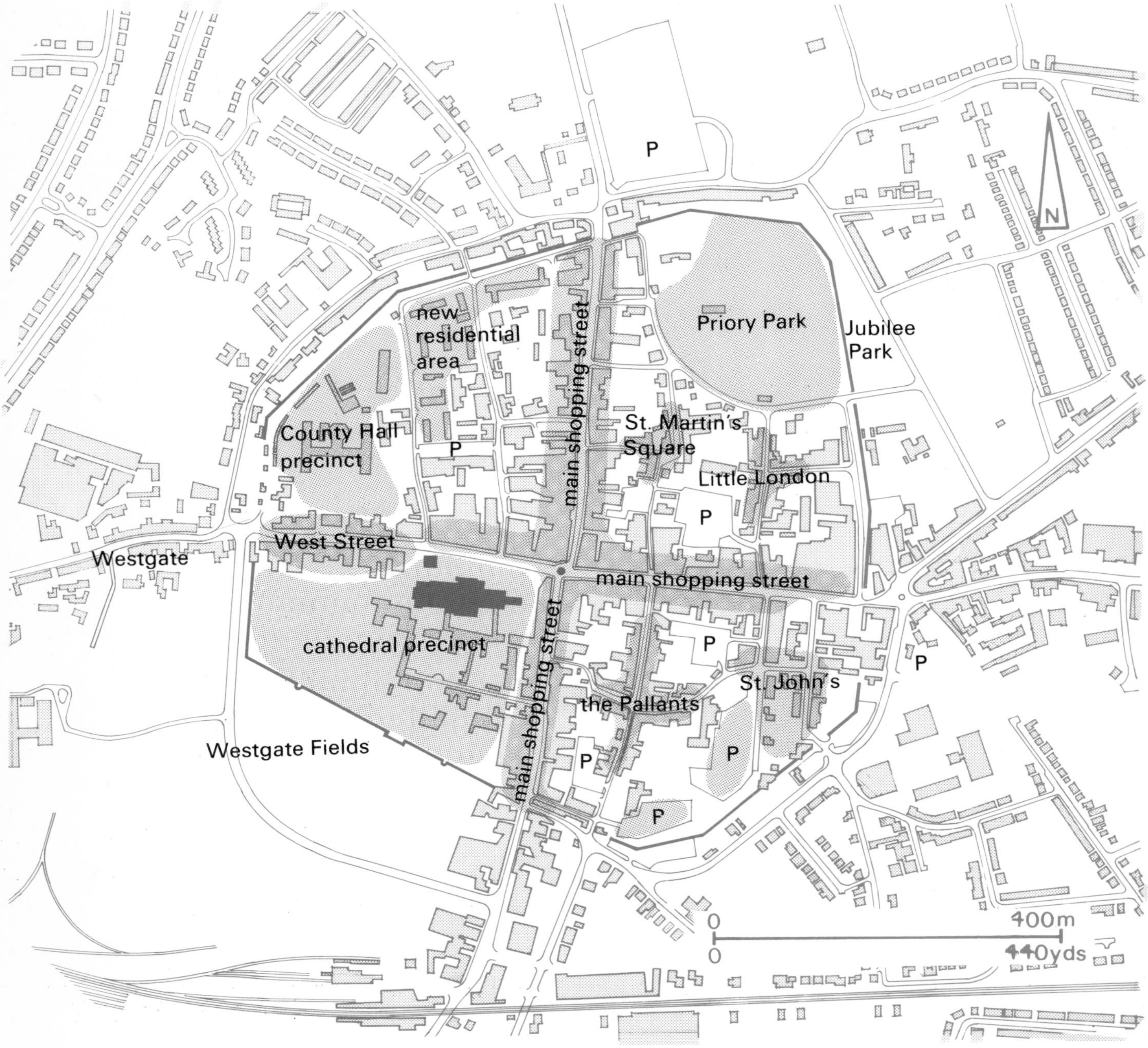

Environmental areas

5.15   On the basis of the criteria mentioned above (5.03), several environmental areas can be identified (fig. 41), and five have special quality. These are:
(a) The four main shopping streets, converging at the Cross
(b) The Cathedral Precinct
(c) The Pallants
(d) St. Martin's Square
(e) Little London

The four main shopping streets, converging at the Cross

5.16   These do not form an exact cross, since North Street is offset slightly to the east, while West Street and East Street make a continuous line (3.06). The Cross closes the view along East, West and South Streets but not along North Street. The frontages vary in alignment in many places, and each street has its own distinctive quality.

5.17   East Street is the least interesting, architecturally, of the four main streets. Of the relatively few buildings which have much individual distinction, the most notable is a cinema (formerly the Corn Exchange (2.16)) with a projecting Doric portico. However the street frontages form the frame to a superb view of the Bell Tower rising behind the Cross with the foliage of trees in between, and the top of the cathedral spire seen above the buildings obliquely on the left (fig. 43). The street has some of the bigger shops, the five principal banks and a variety of smaller shops, the shopping frontages becoming less continuous towards the eastern end.

5.18   North Street has far more architectural character. It begins quite narrowly near the Cross, but widens northwards, with a recession of the eastern frontage, in a very gentle concave curve. The eye is drawn along the varied facades, including that of the former St. Olave's Church (2.09) with its shingled spirelet, to the Georgian Council House (2.16) projecting over the pavement. Beyond this the street narrows, with a succession of excellent buildings, several of them bow-windowed, to a marked closing in at the site of the North Gate (fig. 42). The shopping pattern is very much as in East Street, with some large and many smaller shops, thinning out towards the north end, where one of the city's two principal hotels is situated. This street was further enhanced by the improvement scheme initiated in 1962 (4.43).

5.19   West Street is different, because the south side is open to the cathedral, with an intervening grassed area, a walkway and trees (5.14). The post office, the city's main department store and the other principal hotel face the cathedral on the north side of the street. West of the cathedral, more of the buildings are used for residential or office purposes than for shops.

5.20   South Street is generally narrower and more varied in the scale and character of its buildings than the other streets. Most of the shops are medium to small in size and continue, intermixed with offices and other uses, into Southgate beyond the line of the wall, as far as the bus and railway stations.

42 *North Street* (shopping) *. . . with a succession of excellent buildings* (5.18)

43 *view of the Bell Tower . . . the Cross . . . the cathedral spire* (5.17)

44 *the cathedral precinct . . . there is a convenient network of footways* (5.21)

45 *a small intimate square* (St. Martin's Square) *. . . is still residential* (5.23)

The Cathedral Precinct

5.21   The cathedral precinct is a small enclave between the cathedral and the city wall, and behind the commercialised frontage to South Street (2.04). Its traditional, very high environmental quality has remained unimpaired by bad building or incongruous uses. Traffic is restricted to one cul-de-sac, but there is a convenient network of footways inter-connecting with the cloister (fig. 44). The houses are of medieval to modern date and very varied in style and texture. (2.15). They are sited informally, some of them close to the cathedral, others in spacious gardens which abut onto the wall, most notably the Bishop's Palace which has many fine trees in its large grounds. The Vicars' Close, originally a medieval quadrangle (2.04), reduced in area in 1825 (6.28), adjoins the Canon Gate which forms the entrance to the precinct from South Street. The quiet of the precinct provides an impressive and immediate contrast to the bustle of the adjoining shopping streets.

The Pallants

5.22   This was the former 'palatinate' (2.06) with a cross pattern of streets reflecting, on a smaller scale, the city's main street pattern. In the eighteenth century it was a fashionable residential area, and its architectural character today is almost entirely Georgian (2.15). The houses are, in almost equal measure, still occupied residentially or used as professional offices. Because of the careful maintenance of the external appearance of those houses which have been converted to offices, the area retains a dominantly residential character.

St. Martin's Square

5.23   This area is given special distinction by the form of its street pattern, as well as the architectural quality and high standard of maintenance of most of its predominantly Georgian houses. A tapering street links at its widest end with a small, intimate square from which a narrow, gently curving street leads into North Street. Most of the area is still residential (fig. 45). The medieval St. Mary's Hospital (2.10) is the dominating feature in the area, although the main building is actually set back behind the forebuilding which follows the line of the frontage to St. Martin's Square.

Little London

5.24   Little London is a narrow, slightly winding street with terraces of houses and cottages, many of them recently improved. From it another street leads to the city wall, and at the junction of the two streets a small square has been successfully formed as a forecourt to the recently established museum (3.36), making an effective focal point to this environment (fig. 46).

5.25   There are many other areas in the city centre which can be identified for their distinctive environmental qualities; Westgate and St. Pancras (outside the former city gates), both predominantly Georgian and residential in character; St. John's Street (2.15), another Georgian street within the city walls partly put to office uses and partly residential; Priory Park, dominated by the medieval friars' church (2.26); the County Hall enclave (2.34); and two small areas of recent residential development in the north-west quadrant.

Finally, some of the city's central car parks have been treated in such a way (3.11) that they form a positive contrast in environment from the close-built streets which surround them.

5.26   Chichester is particularly interesting because it contains so many areas of special distinction, each with its own character and atmosphere, and in such close proximity to each other, producing a sequence of unusual variety for such a compact city.

Environmental appraisal

5.27   In making an appraisal of the quality of environment of any section of a town, it is necessary to take into account many variable factors, including some which require essentially subjective judgements (5.03). It may be found valuable, in assessing and comparing the environmental qualities of different areas of a town, to set out all the possible criteria for assessment and comparison on a check list. This would include land and building uses, architectural and townscape considerations, traffic, both moving and stationary, and the movements of people. Assessments would be on a 'points' basis, according to a predetermined system, so ensuring a reasonably objective basis for the comparisons (fig. 47). Such a method could be used not only to compare different areas within a town, but also, in a relatively unfamiliar area, to assess the major problems and therefore to estimate planning priorities. It would be advisable for more than one surveyor to study each area and compile the assessment, in order to reduce any possible personal bias.

5.28   This method of appraisal was not used in Chichester except to test its validity, since considerable work had already been carried out at various times on many of the relevant aspects. In an area where no previous studies of this sort have been made, such a method of appraisal would provide a relatively quick way of ensuring a systematic and complete environmental survey which reduces reliance on individual subjective judgments.

47   *environmental appraisal. . . on a 'points' basis (5.27)*

ENVIRONMENTAL APPRAISAL OF TOWN CENTRE

town:
district:
date:
time:
surveyor:
block no:

category	item	+ 3	+ 2	+ 1	neutral	− 1	− 2	− 3	totals + / −	comments
general planning aspects	land use			well related	acceptable	occasional noise, smell	frequent noise, smell			
visual aspects	structural quality			good	unexceptional	poor	very poor			
	aesthetic quality	excellent	very good	good	unexceptional	poor	very poor			
	relation to adj. area			well related	acceptable	poorly related				
	street scale			good	acceptable	becoming spoilt	scale lost			
	landscaping			positive contribution	appropriate	inadequate treatment	inappropriate treatment			
	street furniture			noticeably good	acceptable	some improvement needed	radical improvement needed			
	advertisements			good	no visual conflict	some clutter	much clutter			
traffic (moving)	danger to pedestrians				none	occasional	constant			
	delay to pedestrians				none	occasional	constant			
	noise				acceptable	difficult to converse	impossible to converse			
	fumes				none	occasional	constant			
	damage to property				none	some damage	considerable damage			
	visual intrusion				none	occasional visual barrier	frequent visual barrier			
traffic (parked)	danger to pedestrians				none	occasional	frequent			
	adequacy of parking				adequate	inadequate for callers	inadequate for the use, or callers			
	adequacy of servicing				adequate	rear access to half of all shops	rear access to one quarter of all shops	street loading only		
people	pedestrian flow			enough people to add vitality	unexceptional	occasionally too many or too few	frequently too many or too few			
	sub totals									
	TOTAL									

Note for surveyors

structural quality
- good — most buildings well maintained
- poor — most buildings show evidence of structural defects or are poorly maintained
- very poor — predominance of buildings in very poor condition

aesthetic quality
- excellent — all buildings exceptionally good
- very good — predominance of buildings with at least some good features
- good — some buildings with at least some good features
- poor — many buildings of poor quality, none of merit
- very poor — all buildings of poor quality

48 *a section of the city was selected for special study . . . (5.29)*

The choice of the Study Area

5.29 Following the analysis of the visual survey of street scenes in the city centre (4.35), a section of the city, eighteen acres in extent, was selected for special study (fig. 48). This section includes South Street, the area around the Cross, the Pallants, and adjoining open spaces bordering the city wall. The area was chosen because it contains three very characteristic types of environment :

(a) Part of the shopping area, where a fairly high degree of pressure for change could be expected. Of the main streets, South Street (5.20) was preferred because, unlike West Street, it is predominantly a shopping street; unlike East Street, it contains a considerable number of historic buildings; and unlike North Street, it has not been the subject of any previous improvement scheme (4.44).

(b) Office and residential area. The Pallants, a well defined office and residential area, (5.22) immediately adjoins South Street, and was considered an excellent area for study because it is an environment of very special distinction, for which no comprehensive improvement has been carried out.

(c) Open area. The open area between the Pallants and the city wall is included in the Study Area since it gave the opportunity for studying planning problems relating to urban open spaces.

6 Survey and analysis of the Study Area

6.01   The survey material, and the analysis of the findings, is presented in four main stages.

6.02   Firstly, there is a description of the townscape of the three main sectors of the Study Area, based on the survey previously carried out for the city centre as a whole (6.04). Secondly, the material obtained from the detailed survey of the Study Area is set out, and analysed (6.21). This is followed by further consideration of the traffic conditions, and an attempt to establish environmental capacity (6.95). Finally, there is an analysis of the present and potential environmental pattern of the area (6.109).

6.03   Captain Wynne's Map of 1875 shows the area in great clarity (2.25) (fig. 49).   The pattern of streets and buildings has not greatly altered since then, but the form and layout of the extensive spaces in the area, which were mainly private gardens or grounds in 1875, have undergone considerable change (6.112).

Townscape survey

6.04   Following the Review of the Development Plan (4.35) a townscape survey of the city centre was carried out in order to assess the contribution to the environment of individual buildings, groups of buildings, viewpoints, the form of spaces and their relationship to buildings, trees, street furniture, and other incidental features which are significant in the urban scene. Photographs were taken and sketches made with comments regarding the effects on the environment, positive or detrimental, of each feature.

South Street and the Cross

6.05   South Street (5.29) is still generally harmonious in scale, architectural style and building materials (5.20), and given distinction by a few notable landmarks.

6.06   The predominant scale is that of three domestic storeys, but there is considerable variation. The relatively few older buildings which are markedly smaller or larger in scale than the majority do not disturb the overall harmony (3.09). Most have roof-lines parallel to the street, with eaves, cornices or parapets, but a few have gable ends, again providing interesting incidental variations which are not disturbing to the total effect. Although several of the buildings in the street retain pre-Georgian external features, and some have been rebuilt in modern times, the prevailing character is Georgian. Red brick is less dominant than in some other parts of central Chichester; many of the buildings have stuccoed or rendered facades, which are harmonious with the rest. Disharmony to the total effect is caused by a few unsatis-

49 *Captain Wynne's map of 1875 shows the* (Study)
area in great clarity (6.03)

This map is also of use for the identification of streets and certain individual
buildings mentioned in the following chapters.

50 *originally formed part of Vicars' Close* (western side) (6.08)

51 *which have changed little outwardly in the last hundred years or more* (6.08)

factory recent buildings or alterations to older buildings, and by some of the street furniture. Street lamps, however, are relatively inconspicuous, being bracketed from buildings. Traffic signs and the recently introduced yellow lines are specially intrusive visually.

6.07 In describing the detailed features of the street it is convenient to consider it in three sections. The southernmost section is fairly narrow and slightly curving, with some distinctive, mainly Georgian, facades in conspicuous positions (6.31). It is narrowest at the site of the South Gate (3.06) where buildings, seen in perspective, give definition to the southward view.

6.08 The street widens in its middle section, with an irregular range of buildings on the western side (fig. 52) which originally formed part of the Vicars' Close (6.28) and which have changed little outwardly in the last hundred years or more (figs. 50 and 51). The Canon Gate leads into the cathedral precinct (5.21) (fig. 53), and beside the Vicars' Hall a small passageway gives access to the space adjoining the east end of the cathedral.

6.09 Beyond the Vicars' Hall the western frontage juts out, and the view along the northernmost section of the street is closed effectively by the Cross, backed by fairly tall buildings.

6.10 Although the cathedral spire is the dominant feature of the city as a whole, the Cross (6.27) is the pivot of the four main streets. The townscape setting of the Cross, and its visual relationship to the varied buildings and spaces around, seem very different from each direction (5.16). Only the spire of the cathedral is visible from South Street, but the whole building comes into view at the Cross, set beyond the open space on the south side of West Street (5.19).

52 *an irregular range of buildings on the western side* (of South Street) (6.08)

Nos. 13 - 24

Nos. 1- 13

Nos. 1- 13   facades to cathedral precinct

The Pallants

6.11   The Pallants have been described as 'a town within a city' (2.06). The whole environment has a special quality of its own, with its cruciform street pattern of medieval origin (2.06), and its almost completely Georgian appearance. The predominant tone is that of red brick, but a few of the buildings are faced in other materials (notably stucco), providing acceptable contrasts. The scale is set by the substantial three-storeyed town houses which are specially conspicuous at the crossroads in the centre of the area, although in many parts of the Pallants the buildings are quite small and of two storeys. The townscape effects vary, because of the differing relationships between the buildings and the streets, with their changing widths and alignments; but the general impression is that of a close-knit urban environment, in very marked contrast to the openness of the area immediately to the south-east (6.19).

6.12   The entrance to the area from South Street is relatively inconspicuous. The first stretch of West Pallant is narrow, and visually closed by the flint façade of All Saints-in-the-Pallant (2.09). The effect of the townscape here is spoilt by the gaps in the frontages mainly used for car parking. The street curves twice and then widens and is given dignity by large, though differing, Georgian (or Georgian fronted) houses on the south side, and buildings of more varied scale on the north side. The view eastwards is partly closed by the very fine

Pallant House (2.15), with the narrow East Pallant leading beside it. The view back along West Pallant is marred, most unfortunately, by the back elevations of buildings in South Street, notably the former cinema converted into a supermarket (6.40), but is dominated by the cathedral spire rising magnificently above the lower buildings in the foreground. An old brick and timber outbuilding is significantly placed on the curve towards the west end of the street.

6.13   North Pallant is a narrow street, lined continuously with various Georgian houses of large to medium size (fig. 54). Those on the eastern side are seen well in perspective from either end.

6.14   East Pallant begins with a gentle northward curve, a fine row of large Georgian houses being seen in perspective on the outside of the curve. Unfortunately, as in part of West Pallant, the effect is marred on the other side by gaps between buildings used for parking cars (fig. 55). Part of East Pallant House (6.30), with its rather unattractive recent additions, half closes the view along the first stretch of the street. The street then bends and comes into an area where the townscape is less clearly defined. There are well placed Georgian cottages on the north side of the street, but on the opposite side is the car parking area which was formerly part of the grounds of East Pallant House (6.19).

6.15   South Pallant is a narrow street where the buildings are mostly of a smaller scale than elsewhere in the Pallants. The eastern frontage ends pleasantly with the wooded grounds of Cawley Priory (6.30). On the western side there are gaps in the frontage (forming about 45% of its length) particularly towards the southern end, so that the visual coherence of the street is weakened.

6.16   Theatre Lane is a short narrow street with a variety of buildings, including Georgian cottages and recently erected offices. It joins South Street near its southern end (fig. 56).

6.17   Although buildings line the streets almost continuously in the mainly built up part of the Pallants area, the gaps used for car parking break this continuity, spoil the scale of the streets and sometimes give views of servicing areas which are inappropriate to the character of a largely residential area. Examples of this have been described in West Pallant (6.12), East Pallant (6.14) and South Pallant (6.15).

6.18   The Pallants retain several metal lamp standards which are relatively harmonious. Overhead wires are a conspicuous element in South Pallant. Traffic signs and road markings are specially intrusive, as in South Street (6.06).

54   *North Pallant is . . . lined continuously with various Georgian houses (6.13)*

55 *East Pallant . . . is marred . . . by gaps . . . used for parking cars* (6.14)

56 *Theatre Lane is a short narrow street with a variety of buildings* (6.16)

The open areas

6.19 The south-eastern part of the Study Area consists of the former grounds of East Pallant House and Cawley Priory (6.56), now partly used for car parking (6.80). Although many fine trees remain, the former park-like atmosphere of the area has been almost entirely lost, due to the unbroken asphalted expanse of the car park, which, although covering only about half of the total area, has been allowed to become the dominant element (fig. 57). Thus the city wall and adjacent Georgian houses are now seen beyond a foreground of vehicles or bleak asphalt. The lighting standards, traffic signs and kiosks in the parking area are visually intrusive.

6.20 The smaller car parks west of Baffin's Lane and west of South Pallant (6.80) are more attractively laid out. Trees (both old and recently planted) and old boundary walls make positive contributions to the quality of the environment. Here too, however, traffic signs and kiosks are visually jarring elements (fig. 58).

57 *the unbroken asphalted expanse of the car park . . . the dominant element (6.19)*

58 *trees . . . and old boundary walls make positive contributions to the quality of the environment . . . traffic signs . . . are visually jarring elements (6.20)*

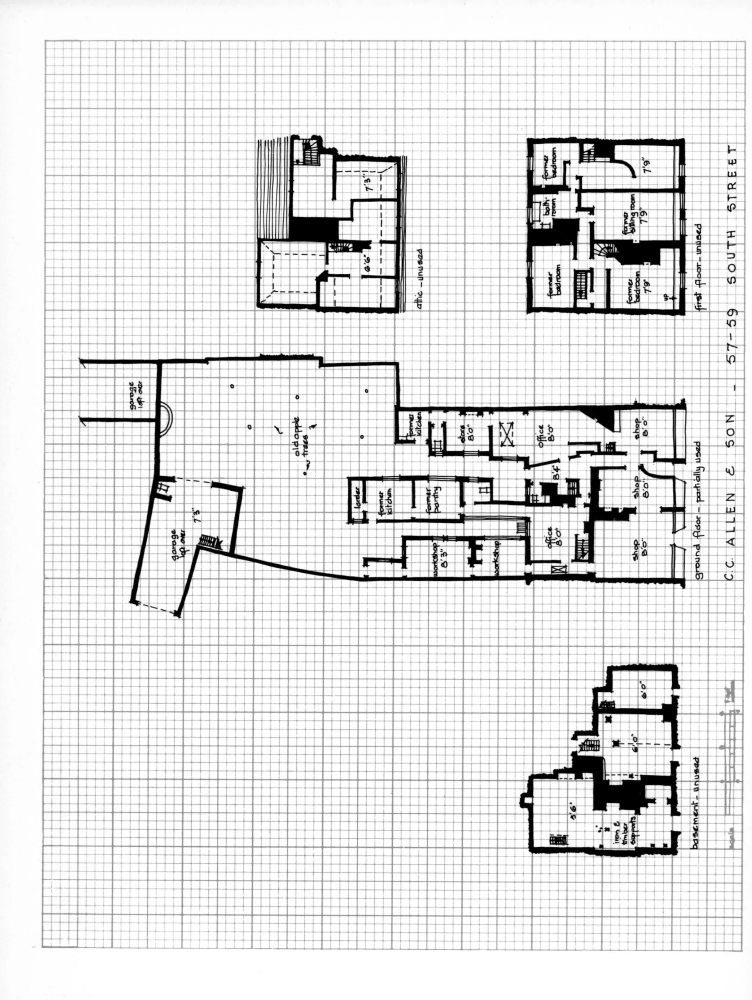

attic - unused

7'3"

6'6"

former
bedroom

bath
room

7'9"

former
sitting room
7'9"

former
bedroom

former
bedroom
7'9"

up

first floor - unused

garage
loft over

old apple
trees

garage
loft over
7'3"

larder

former
kitchen

former
pantry

workshop
8'3"

workshop

former
kitchen

store
8'0"

office

office
8'0"

8'4"

shop
8'0"

shop
8'0"

office
8'0"

shop
8'0"

ground floor - partially used

6'0"

6'0"

5'6"

iron &
timber
supports

basement - unused

scale

C.C. ALLEN & SON — 57-59 SOUTH STREET

78

Survey of individual buildings and spaces

6.21   The purpose of the detailed survey of all the properties in the Study Area was to establish facts from which could be judged the positive and potential qualities of this section of the city, to identify problems which have arisen, or are likely to arise, within it, and to relate these to the Conservation Area (5.01) as a whole.

6.22   The occupants of all properties in the Study Area were advised by letter of the nature of the survey and when it was to be undertaken. They were asked to co-operate by allowing the surveyors to make plans of their properties, note the general condition of structures, and record special features. A form was enclosed which asked for details of tenure, and invited comments on problems of access, garaging, etc. A shopping survey on a sample basis for the whole city had already been carried out in connection with the Reviewed Development Plan, and this had covered certain properties in the Study Area. The owners and occupiers of the shops which had not been covered in the previous survey were asked to give appropriate information, including details of numbers and types of servicing vehicles, delivery vehicles and staff movement. All the properties were then visited by the surveyors, who collected the forms previously sent, and drew one-sixteenth scale sketch plans on field survey sheets (fig. 59). The response, on the part of the owners and occupiers, was virtually 100%. The surveyors also recorded, on architectural assessment forms (fig. 60) factors of structural and architectural significance, including the relationship of buildings to each other. These forms included provision for reassessing the architectural quality of buildings included in the statutory list of buildings of special architectural or historical interest so that recommendations could be made for any amendments which were considered to be necessary. The survey was carried out in April/May 1967.

6.23   The material obtained in the survey was analysed under eight headings:
(a) Architectural quality, including age, style, construction and detailed features (6.24)
(b) Use of buildings and land (6.24)
(c) Condition and maintenance (6.61)
(d) Population, residential and working (6.76)
(e) Traffic generation, including access, parking, servicing (6.79)
(f) Tenure, whether freehold, leasehold, public land, etc. (6.88)
(g) Financial aspects (6.91)
(h) Pressures, economic and social (6.92)

Architectural qualities, including age, style and construction
(keys 9, 10 and 11)

6.24   The buildings in the Study Area are very varied in style, height and age. Many buildings with Georgian fronts are of earlier origin (2.15), and many which are substantially Georgian or earlier have had considerable later additions or alterations.

6.25   Because many buildings are of composite date, it is not always possible to make firm dividing lines between different periods. They are therefore treated broadly under the following headings:
(a) Medieval buildings
(b) Early domestic buildings
(c) Georgian buildings
(d) Victorian buildings
(e) Modern buildings

	external - front	external - rear	basement	ground floor	first floor	second floor	third floor	attic
survey date								
surveyed by								
address of property								
architectural / group value								
retain / marginal / alter / demolish								
existing grade								
suggested grade								

	external - front	external - rear	basement	ground floor	first floor	second floor	third floor	attic
construction type material original / rebuilt alterations/additions dates								
condition good / medium / poor repairs immediate / long term								
planning satisfactory / improvements								
features of note								
general comments								
historical notes								
no. and type occupants								

Medieval buildings

6.26   The flint built thirteenth century church of All Saints-in-the-Pallants is the oldest building in the Study Area which remains substantially in its original form (fig. 61). It is typical of the once numerous medieval parish churches in the city (2.09), a simple rectangle with lancet windows and a plain moulded doorway. It originally had a wooden spirelet over the western gable, which was replaced by the present stone bellcote in the nineteenth century.

6.27   The Cross, built in 1501 (2.05), was originally constructed of Caen stone. Because of the deterioration of the stonework, much of the structure has had to be renewed, particularly in recent times. The uppermost part of the Cross was replaced by the present cupola in 1729 (2.16).

6.28   The middle part of the western frontage to South Street is occupied by buildings which are medieval in origin and formed part of the College of the Vicars Choral, later Vicars' Close (2.04) (fig. 62). This was originally a rectangular courtyard with parallel ranges of buildings on the longer sides, one of which backed onto South Street, with the Vicars' Hall at the northern end. In 1825, the courtyard was subdivided by a wall, and the eastern range, which had previously been very much altered and extended, particularly in Georgian times, was converted into shop premises fronting South Street. The Vicars' Hall itself is a very fine fourteenth century stone built hall with a late twelfth century vaulted undercroft, but with an eighteenth century façade to South Street.

61   *the flint thirteenth century church of All Saints-in-the-Pallant* (6.26)

62   *buildings which are medieval in origin . . . Vicars'
Close* (6.28)

63   *the Punch House . . .* (has a) *fine Elizabethan
ceiling* (6.29)

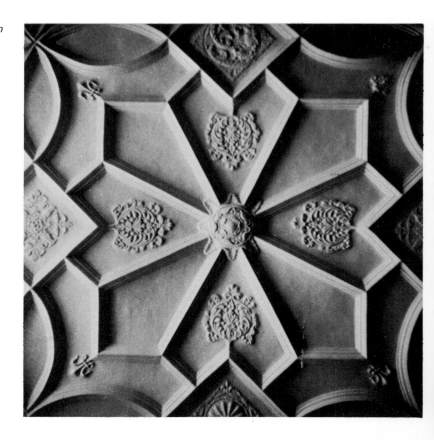

64 *several of the larger houses . . . have fine staircases*
(6.30)

Early domestic buildings

6.29 Many of the buildings in South Street and the Pallants with Georgian or later fronts are basically timber framed houses of late medieval, Tudor or early seventeenth century date. Occasionally, early external walling with lath and plaster over timber framing survives. Some buildings have notable pre-Georgian panelling and other features inside. 'The Punch House' (Royal Arms) and the adjoining shop have fine Elizabethan ceilings (fig. 63). Behind one property on the east side of South Street is a former granary of timber and brick, probably of seventeenth century date, which is in poor condition.

Georgian buildings

6.30 The eighteenth century buildings are mainly in red brick; those of the early nineteenth century are frequently stuccoed (3.10). Larger and medium sized Georgian houses are very numerous in the Pallants. The finest is Pallant House, built in 1712 (2.15) (fig. 65), which retains its stone gate piers supporting ostriches (the emblem of the family which originally lived there), and decorative iron railings. The other houses in the area show a great variety of classical door cases, and many have the locally characteristic cornices, with brick-work in dentil patterns. The main parts of the two larger detached houses in the area are Georgian but both have been much added to, Cawley Priory in the nineteenth century when it was still a residence and East Pallant House since its conversion to offices during the present century. Several of the larger houses, particularly in the Pallants, have fine staircases (fig. 64), panelling and other internal features.

6.31 In South Street most of the Georgian buildings have modern shop fronts in their ground storeys but some, towards the southern end, remain relatively little altered externally. The former Literary and Philosophical Society (2.16), now a club, is a large early eighteenth century house which, though altered in the mid-nineteenth century when the front was stuccoed, retains its original proportions. Flint House has an attractive flint facade (3.10), but the adjoining Old Theatre (6.37) has been altered by the insertion of a shop front (fig. 66).

6.32 Some of the medium-sized eighteenth century houses in South Street, nearly all much altered, were of a type which was fairly common in the main streets of Chichester. They usually had three main storeys, with attic and basement, but some had one storey less. They had two principal rooms (front and rear) on the ground floor with a staircase in between, and a rear extension about half as wide as the house. There were two similarly placed rooms on the first floor. Where the street frontage had three main storeys, the roof slope at the rear often began at second floor level, so that the rear elevation had two main storeys and a broad sweeping roof with dormer windows lighting the second floor. Attics were lit by dormer windows over the main frontages. Roofs were simply constructed and covered with clay pegged tiles, but were often complicated in the arrangement of their pitches. Valleys between roof slopes and back gutters to low parapets were common features.

6.33 Houses of this type were generally fronted with brick to a thickness of nine inches and often rendered. Interior walls (including party walls) were usually timber framed and only four inches thick. Sometimes this internal framework survived from before the eighteenth century (6.24) but it seems that partition walls continued to be built in timber framing well into the Georgian period. Framing was generally in a rectangular pattern, with diagonal braces, infilled with brick on

65 *Pallant House, built in 1712* (6.30)

66 *the former Literary and Philosophical Society (in a large eighteenth century house) . . . Flint House . . . the adjoining Old Theatre* (6.31)

the lower floors but often covered with tarred hessian and papered or decorated on the upper floors. There were often no partitions between properties in the roof space.

6.34 Like most properties in the main streets, these typical houses had basements with brick or stone flagged floors, and coal cellars extending under the footpaths which were sometimes connected to tunnels running under the streets. Wells and cesspools opening from the basement were common features. Load bearing walls below ground level were usually of solid flint (about two feet thick), but the bases of party walls, which were up to about three feet in thickness were often only flint faced, with earth or rubble cores. These usually extended no more than six or nine inches below basement floor level, resting on the black earth which underlies Chichester for depths varying from fourteen feet in the centre of the city to four feet on the fringes of the central area, below which is load bearing gravel. The water table is approximately twenty feet below ground level.

6.35 Where houses of this basic traditional type remain they have usually been greatly altered at ground floor level, and extensions have often been built at the rear as a result of commercial pressures (6.43) (fig. 69). Some of these old houses however, are still largely in their original condition, both internally and externally, at upper levels and in the basements.

6.36 There are many Georgian houses of smaller scale in the Pallants area; the most typical have simple brick elevations with gable-hooded doorways and dentil patterning in the brickwork under the eaves.

6.37 There are two notable Georgian buildings of non-domestic character. The Old Theatre, built in 1791 (2.16), retains the upper part of its original pedimented frontage (6.31) but the interior has been altered. The former Unitarian Chapel of 1721, with its pleasant brick exterior (2.17), retains much of its original internal character.

Victorian buildings

6.38 There is no specially notable Victorian architecture in the Study Area. The former Post Office, now an estate agent's office, is a building of classical proportions and strong detailing, the qualities of which have been fully brought out with recent alterations and redecorations (fig. 67).

6.39 Some of the surviving shop fronts of the period have consider-able charm (fig. 68).

Modern buildings

6.40 The most sensitively designed recent building in the Study Area is a shop by Sir Hugh Casson, near the Cross (4.45). It is not imitative in style, but respects the predominantly Georgian character of its surroudings with its carefully considered scale and proportions, its texture and its colour, making no violent contrast (fig. 70). Many inter-war and post-war buildings in the Study Area are neo-Georgian, but none are convincing works in this imitative style. Other recent build-ings are in various nondescript styles; the most intrusive, in scale and design, is an inter-war cinema in South Street (3.35), now converted into a supermarket.

6.41 Recent alterations and redecorations of properties in South Street have sometimes resulted in improvements, but many of the present shop fronts and fascias are disruptive to the harmony of the street. Such disruption may be due to:

67 *the former Post Office . . . is a building of classical proportions* (6.38)

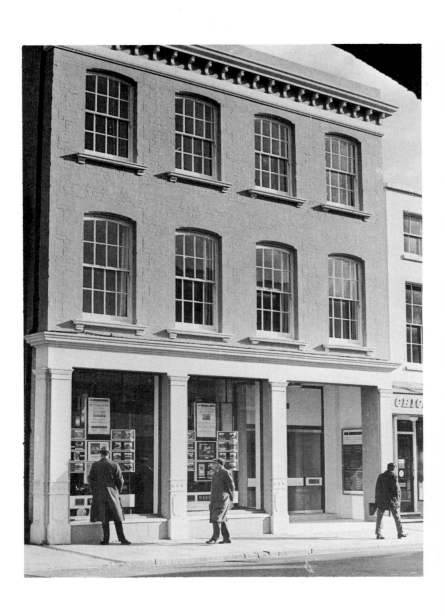

68 *some of the surviving shop fronts ... have considerable charm* (6.39)

69 *extensions have often been built at the rear as a result of commercial pressures* (6.35)

70 *a shop . . . near the Cross . . . respects the predominantly Georgian character of its surroundings (6.40)*

71 *understandable reluctance to use upper floors*
(6.48)

(a) Too great a horizontal emphasis, in a street where the architectural rhythm is largely determined by repeated small scale features with vertical emphasis (5.11).

(b) Large expanses of plate glass which are not satisfactorily related, in their proportions, to the rest of the buildings within which they are set.

(c) Fascias which are excessively wide, or too high on the frontages of the buildings.

(d) The use of facing materials or paint of inappropriate texture or colour.

(e) Conspicuous and unsightly downpipes, light boxes and other features affixed to the facades.

(f) Unsightly advertisements placed on the insides of windows, which are very conspicuous from the street.

6.42   Where upper floors are used for storage or other commercial purposes, stored materials, or even lighting fittings, are sometimes unduly conspicuous from the street.

6.43   Some back elevations of recent buildings are unsightly. New additions have often been made to the backs of old buildings, sometimes with unsatisfactory materials which are visually detrimental (6.35).

Use of buildings and land (key 7)

6.44   The Study Area as a whole contains a great variety of uses. Retail and other commercial uses are concentrated in South Street and in the area around the Cross; residential and professional office uses are found in the Pallants, and the rest comprises mainly open areas.

The shopping area
6.45   Nearly all the properties along South Street and around the Cross are used for retail purposes (including restaurants and public houses) or office purposes at ground floor level; the main exceptions are the Congregational Church and a club (6.31).

6.46   The shops in the Study Area provide a fairly representative selection of the types of retail trade within the central area, although there is a rather smaller proportion of the larger types of shop in the Study Area than in the shopping centre as a whole (3.29). A branch of a multiple chemist, a supermarket (6.40) and a motor showroom are the largest in the Study Area. Office uses, such as building societies, estate agents and professional offices are, typically, interspersed with the shopping uses. There is a higher proportion of non-retail uses towards the southern end of South Street (5.20).

6.47   A small proportion of the shops, notably clothing, footwear and furniture shops, have selling space on the first floors, and there are a few instances of separate retail businesses (such as restaurants and hairdressers) above ground level. Basements are occasionally used for additional sales space.

6.48   Retail storage and staff facilities tend to be concentrated on the ground floors (6.35), adjoining the main selling space, or on first floors. There is an understandable reluctance to use upper floors for storage unless insufficient space is available at lower levels (fig. 71). In a few cases, however, upper floors are intensively used for storage (6.73).

72 *a few of the professional office premises have unused accommodation in attics* (6.54)

73 *some properties . . . had no unbuilt land* (6.56)

6.49 Office uses are more readily accommodated on upper floors, and there are instances of separate office accommodation above shops.

6.50 About a quarter of the properties in South Street and around the Cross have residential accommodation on the first floor (6.76). Most of this is occupied by people connected with the businesses on the premises, although there are a few instances of upper floors being occupied independently as flats. Very little of the residential accommodation on upper floors has separate access; in most cases it can be reached only through the non-residential parts of the properties.

6.51 Many properties have unused accommodation in upper floors and attics. Two properties were unoccupied at the time of the Survey; one was being converted to office use, and the other had a planning permission for a similar conversion. Two other properties were in process of rebuilding.

The Pallants
6.52 Slightly over half of the properties are in residential use (6.77) and the remainder are used as offices, except for one shop, a club, an auction room (6.60) and two premises occupied by funeral directors. Three premises were empty at the time of the Survey, being offered either for sale or for letting.

6.53 The office uses tend to be found in the larger premises. The three largest of the former houses in the area, Pallant House, East Pallant House and Cawley Priory (6.30) are used as administrative offices for national and local authorities, as is also an inter-war neo-Georgian building adjacent to Pallant House. There is one recently built block of new office premises on the north side of Theatre Lane.

6.54 Many of the larger Georgian town houses are well converted to professional offices (5.22). A typical pattern for these houses is for the ground floor to be used for reception and the principals' offices, the first floor for partners' and general offices, the upper floors for typists and the basements for storage. The pattern varies in detail; in many instances a single property is shared by more than one firm. A few of the professional office premises have unused accommodation in attics (fig. 72) or basements.

6.55 Although some of the larger houses are still in residential occupation (one is a students' hostel, 6.76), the majority of the residential properties in the area are medium-sized or smaller, particularly in South Pallant and at the eastern end of East Pallant. The large Georgian house in West Pallant which adjoins the rear servicing area of the supermarket (6.86) has ceased to be used as a single domestic unit and is now divided into several flats.

Space about buildings (key 5)
6.56 Most of the large and medium sized Georgian and earlier houses had gardens which were generally fairly long and narrow (2.06). Because most of the street frontages were continuously built (on the main streets this has probably been the case since the Middle Ages), these gardens were usually accessible only through the houses, except where they adjoined side streets or lanes. Many smaller houses and cottages had only small gardens or yards, and some properties (as, for example, in the block fronting South Street, east of the cathedral) had no unbuilt land at all (fig. 73). At the opposite extreme there were the large detached houses, Cawley Priory and East Pallant House, in extensive grounds (6.19).

K

74 *as properties became more intensively commercialised, most of the gardens ceased to be maintained* (6.57)

75 *Georgian houses now used as professional offices* (6.59)

6.57 As properties became more intensively commercialised, most of the gardens ceased to be maintained as such, and came to be used as yards, in connection with the business, or were put to little or no use at all (fig. 74). Parts of these spaces were covered by extensions to the premises and by outbuildings. At present, of the five and a half acres of land occupied by the eighty properties in South Street and around the Cross, only about a quarter is unoccupied by buildings.

6.58 Because of the entirely different character of the Pallants, many of the original gardens behind the larger houses fronting the four streets have remained. Parts of former gardens have, however, been absorbed into the car parks west of Baffin's Lane and west of South Pallant (6.80). The former grounds of East Pallant House and Cawley Priory have been very largely converted to car parking use. This part of the Study Area, including the Pallants and the adjoining spaces, contains almost the same number of properties as South Street, but extends for twelve and a half acres, of which nearly two thirds is unoccupied by buildings. The spaciousness of this part of the Study Area contrasts markedly with the closely built South Street area.

Adaptations of old buildings for modern uses
6.59 Most of the old buildings in the Study Area were originally domestic. Conversions to non-domestic uses have sometimes been achieved fairly easily, as in the cases of larger Georgian houses now used as professional offices (fig. 75). In other instances, particularly where medium-sized and small houses have been converted to commercial uses, substantial alterations have been necessary (6.35). Often the original rooms were too small, lighting was unsatisfactory and staircases narrow and badly placed. Attics and other upper rooms did not usually meet modern standards in respect of ventilation, thermal insulation and fire protection. Access to upper floors (where separate uses would be appropriate) is often a problem. Satisfactory conversions of old houses with such disadvantages have, however, been achieved with compromise and ingenuity.

6.60 Conversions of non-domestic buildings to different uses have occurred in the Old Theatre, now an antique market (6.37), the former Unitarian Church, now an auction room (6.37) (fig. 76), and the crypt of the Vicars' Hall (6.28), now used as a restaurant.

76 *the former Unitarian Chapel, now an auction room* (6.60)

77 *roofs are sometimes neglected or inadequately maintained* (6.66)

78 *the standards of maintenance of buildings in the Study Area vary greatly* (6.61)

Condition and maintenance

6.61   The standards of maintenance of buildings in the Study Area vary greatly, depending to a large extent on the types of uses to which the buildings are put, and to the nature of the tenures (6.88) (fig. 78).

6.62   The most consistently high standards are found in the larger Georgian houses used as professional offices (6.52). They are often fully occupied, and kept in good repair for both prestige and economic reasons.

6.63   The widest variations in standards of maintenance were found in the properties with shops on the ground floors, which are often managed and occupied independently of the upper parts of the buildings (6.45). Upper floors, where underused or disused (6.48), are frequently badly maintained. There are, however, a few old buildings in the shopping area where the upper floors are well used, and are kept in good order throughout.

6.64   The poor condition of certain buildings was found to be due to a number of causes which can broadly be grouped into two categories:
(a) Under-use of buildings or parts of buildings
(b) Alterations to buildings, and the effects of new uses and standards

Under-use of buildings or parts of buildings
6.65   Upper floors in the shopping area may be disused or under-used because of lack of commercial pressure to use space above ground level (6.48), because of changing social requirements (fewer people now wish to live in the same premises as the business in which they are engaged) or, in many cases, because of the extent and cost of the structural alterations which would be necessary to bring the accommodation into a suitable condition for a new use, and conform to the standards required under building and fire regulations (6.59).

6.66   When attics or upper floors are disused or little used, their maintenance is often overlooked or delayed over a long period. Roofs are sometimes neglected or inadequately maintained (fig. 77), with consequent slipping of roof tiles, disintegration of flashings and gutters, and deterioration of pointing in chimney stacks (6.32). Fractures often appear around parapets and dormer windows, drainpipes leak, rendering cracks, bricks soften, and damp consequently penetrates, causing a chain reaction with spread of wet rot, mould and dry rot which, in time, may affect whole buildings, including lower storeys which are, in themselves, often well-used and adequately maintained (6.48). Serious structural failure often results. It was found that timbers in many old buildings in the Study Area had been attacked by beetle, and this had often remained undetected because it occurred in parts of the buildings which were disused or little used. However, because of the thickness of the timbers, this was seldom found to be serious.

6.67   The sealing of disused basements, with consequent lack of ventilation, often causes dry rot which can spread rapidly through other parts of buildings.

Alteration to buildings and effects of new uses and standards
6.68   Alterations for commercial use of buildings which were originally domestic in character have sometimes seriously affected their stability. Internal load bearing walls have often been demolished, fireplaces and parts of chimney stacks taken out, and stress-bearing members of timber framed buildings removed to form openings (6.33), (fig. 79) thus transferring thrusts to other parts of the structural

framework, and causing distortion of timbers thereby subjected to excessive stress. Where such over-stressed timbers are tied to load bearing walls, bulging of the walls may result; where they are simply socketed into walls, they may tend to pull away from their sockets. In either case further stresses are set up, which are often followed by settlement or fracture.

6.69   Excavations of basements to lower their floor levels have often resulted in the weakening of walls, which generally extend for only short distances below the original floor levels (6.34). This can be particularly serious where the basement walls consist only of earth in-filling behind flint facings, a form of construction often found under partition walls originally designed to carry little or no superimposed load. Alterations to buildings have sometimes resulted in loads being imposed on partition walls, with consequent pressure on the walls in the basements (which sometimes appear to be more substantial than they are, because of their thickness). As a result the earth infilling is likely to filter out with serious effects on the structure above.

6.70   The introduction of new materials in the course of alterations can have an adverse effect on the stability of buildings, due to differing rates of expansion and compression in old and new materials.

6.71   The stability of buildings can also be seriously affected by demolition of adjacent structures, and this has occurred in the Study Area, where major cracks have appeared in the buildings adjoining a demolition site.

6.72   Even buildings, or additions to buildings, erected during the present century are sometimes in bad condition, because of the use of inferior materials, with consequent shoddy appearance (6.43). In more recent years, however, the use of materials in new construction has been more strictly controlled.

6.73 Upper floors of old buildings are, in some cases, very intensively used for storage. This can result in the weakening of the structures which were not designed to take excessive loads.

6.74 The installation of modern equipment to improve living or working conditions has sometimes been the cause of structural deterioration in old buildings. Heating systems, which reduce the humidity of interiors, may cause shrinkage of timbers which results in a change in the pattern of pressures. Distortion thus caused to floors may lead to restriction on the use of rooms.

6.75 The effects on the stability of structures arising from the causes outlined in the preceding paragraphs are often unforeseen, due to insufficient understanding of the forms of the structures.

Population, residential and working

Residential occupancy
6.76 The total population of the Study Area at the time of the survey was about 170. Of these approximately 70 people lived in South Street and the area around the Cross, nearly all on upper floors of premises used for business purposes on the ground floor, and approximately 100 in the Pallants area, of which fifteen were students in a house in North Pallant used as a hostel for Bishop Otter College (6.55). The survey revealed that the residential population was predominantly in the higher age groups, that several dwellings were occupied by only one person and that there were very few children in the area (the exceptions to the general rule being where accommodation was associated with employment in the Study Area) (6.50). The low occupancy rate of residential properties was clearly indicated by the average household sizes. In the South Street area there was an average of 2.3 persons per household, and in the Pallants only 1.8 persons, compared with an average of 3.1 persons per household in the area covered by the Reviewed Development Plan (4.02).

6.77 The interviews with residents revealed that the Pallants have attracted a residential population which appreciates the unique surroundings and accepts the limitations relating to space and access. By contrast, many of the residents on the upper floors of South Street properties accept relatively poor residential conditions only because accommodation is associated with their employment.

Daytime occupancy
6.78 Altogether about 1130 people are employed in the Study Area, 650 of them in South Street and around the Cross (almost all in shops and offices) (3.29) and about 480 in the Pallants area (mainly in offices) (3.30). Including the resident population, this makes a maximum daytime density in the Pallants area of about 48 persons per acre. Nevertheless, even in daytime, the Pallants area appears quiet and unfrequented, in marked contrast to the bustle of South Street.

Traffic generation (key 3)

6.79 It is of fundamental importance to establish the nature and degree of traffic generation within an area such as the Study Area. Three main sources of traffic generation were found within the area.
(a) Public car parking
(b) Private car parking associated with offices and other establishments, and residential properties
(c) Servicing of shops and other establishments

80 *business premises . . . are serviced directly from the street* (6.86)

81 *the large supermarket is serviced from West Pallant* (6.86)

Public car parking

6.80   At the time of the survey there were 348 parking places in the public car parks in the Study Area, distributed as follows (6.19) :

Adjoining East Pallant House and Cawley Priory	186 places
West of South Pallant	67 places
West of Baffin's Lane	95 places

6.81   In addition, there is a proposal to provide a further 35 places on an extension to the Cawley Priory area.

6.82   Access to the Baffin's Lane car park is from the east end of East Pallant, and the exit leads onto Baffin's Lane (6.20). The South Pallant car park has an access and exit point towards the southern end of South Pallant. The northern part of the East Pallant and Cawley Priory area is served by an access and exit point at the east end of East Pallant, and the southern part is served by the south end of South Pallant. Most of the traffic to and from the car parks does not therefore enter the Pallants area, except at the extremities, where its effect is noticeable on the traffic flows.

Private car parking

6.83   There are about 200 spaces for private car parking, in the open and under cover, in the Study Area. Some of these are in fairly large parking areas, associated with offices or places of assembly, including 74 adjoining East Pallant House, 14 associated with Cawley Priory, and 16 behind the club in South Street (with direct access from the South Pallant car park). Most of the others are on small pieces of land adjoining the streets (6.17). There are very few private domestic garages.

Servicing

6.84   Investigations regarding servicing were made at all business premises within the Study Area, to supplement the earlier survey of shop servicing (4.15). The analysis of the material indicated the considerable scale of the servicing problem within the area.

6.85   It was found that there are about 290 trips generated daily by the business premises in South Street, West Street, North Street and East Street which are within the Study Area. About 70 of these are to premises with a frontage to the proposed pedestrian precinct (i.e. north of Cooper Street) (4.14), with almost half of this total generated by the section to the north east. Of the remainder, about 110 calls are to properties on the west side of South Street and about 100 to properties on the east side.

6.86   Almost all the business premises in South Street and around the Cross are serviced directly from the street (fig. 80). There is no acceptable alternative for those on the west side of South Street (4.16). Seven units on the east side of the street have provision for servicing off the street, although three of these are also partly serviced from the street. The large supermarket (6.40) is serviced from West Pallant, with seriously detrimental effect on the quality of the environment (6.55) (fig. 81).

6.87   In the Pallants, only seven of the offices are serviced off the street, and three of these also use the street for servicing. Some of the private houses in the area have garage or servicing access off the streets.

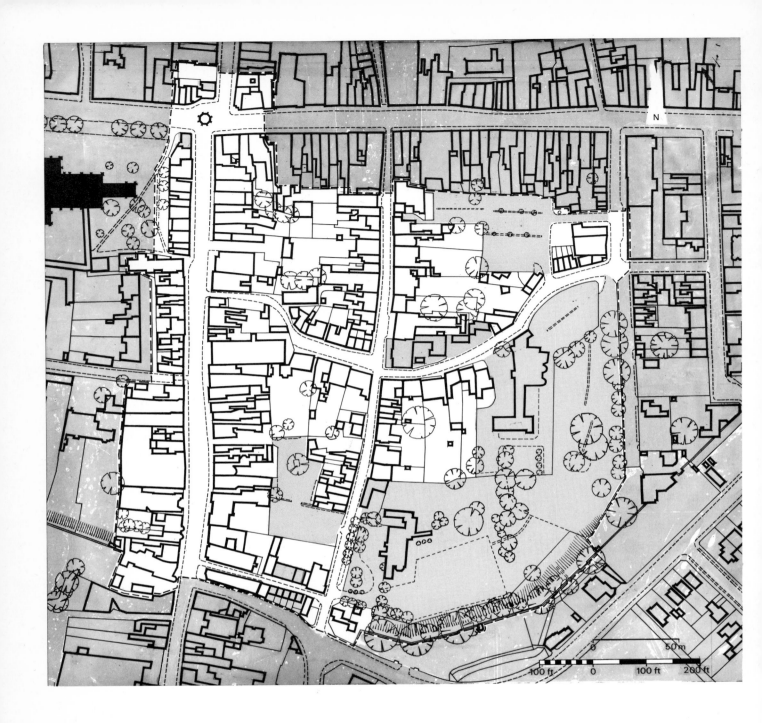

land in public ownership

82 *public bodies own several properties . . . and . .*
most of the open land (in the Study Area) (6.90)

Tenures

6.88 In South Street and around the Cross just over half the properties are leasehold and the remainder are occupied by the free-holders. The only relatively large concentration of land in one ownership in South Street is the block which originally formed part of the Vicars' Close (6.08) which is owned by the Dean and Chapter of the cathedral. This block has remained subdivided into small units each separately let.

6.89 In the Pallants the majority of the properties are occupied by the freeholders.

6.90 Public bodies own several properties in the Study Area, including buildings used as public offices (Cawley Priory, East Pallant House and Pallant House) (6.53) and a few premises elsewhere which are leased to private occupants. Most of the open land in the south-eastern part of the Study Area, including the principal car parking areas (6.80), is in public ownership (fig. 82). The boundary between adjacent pieces of land owned by two public bodies in this area has been rigidly maintained, mainly by a low brick wall which visually breaks the continuity of the open land (6.19) (fig. 83).

Financial aspects

6.91 The material obtained in the survey carried out in the Study Area (6.22) enabled calculations to be made of the floor areas, and included details of leasehold interests (although these were sometimes incomplete or imprecise). With this information, together with rating assessments, the results of property transactions carried out in the area during the last two years, and other incidental data which was obtained, it was possible to make valuations for all the properties in the Study Area (8.17). These form the basis for the calculations of the cost of the recommended development in Chapter 7.

Pressures

6.92 There have been relatively few planning applications for development in the Study Area, the total since 1947 being about 180, excluding minor revisions and modifications. The number submitted has increased by about 50 per cent. in each five-year period. Rather more than half of the applications relate to South Street and the area around the Cross, and these are mainly for alterations and extensions to existing shop premises. The remainder, relating to the Pallants and minor streets, include a number for alterations and extensions to residential and business premises. Applications for change of use from residential to office use have become more numerous in recent years, although the total is still small. There have been few applications for new development in the Study Area.

6.93 Apart from the increase in shop improvements and alterations, and the less marked increase in the number of conversions to office use, it seems that there are no strong commercial pressures in the area. There are, for example, a large number of vacant rooms in upper floors in the Study Area (6.48), but there is little evidence of commercial interest in using this accommodation.

Tourism

6.94 No detailed study was undertaken of the existing and potential importance of tourism in the city, because of the relatively limited time and resources available. A study of coastal facilities* had, however, already been carried out by the County Council as a basis for the formulation of an overall policy (3.24). An increase in the number of tourists in the city would not be likely to add significantly to its planning problems, but would make added justification for proposals which lead to preservation and improvement of the historical environment.

Environmental capacity

Definition and measurement

6.95 In the report *Traffic in Towns* (3.38), Professor Buchanan defined the environmental capacity of a street as a measure of the 'volume and character of the traffic permissible in the street consistent with the maintenance of good environmental conditions'. (5.03) The amount varies greatly with the environmental conditions of each street or area, and is usually well below the straightforward physical capacity of the street to absorb traffic.

6.96 It is very difficult to devise means of determining statistically where the environmental capacity of a street has been exceeded. One method suggested by Professor Buchanan, particularly applicable to roads carrying heavy traffic and passing through environmental areas, was to measure the average length of delay for pedestrians wishing to cross the flows of traffic. If these figures remained below desirable maxima (determined with reference to the environmental and physical conditions of the streets or localities), it would be assumed that the amounts of traffic were acceptable.

*See bibliography: *Coastal Report,* 1966

6.97 Other means of determining the detrimental effects of traffic on the environment are to measure the noise and the degree of atmospheric pollution caused by vehicles. This can be done with appropriate instruments. The effects of vibration, which can affect the stability of buildings as well as the quality of environment, are more difficult to establish.

Environmental capacity in Chichester

6.98 The special historical character of Chichester is such that these methods of measuring environmental capacity are not wholly appropriate for the city's central streets. Delays to traffic in the main streets during the day, caused by the presence of the Cross and a busy pedestrian crossing at the centre of the town, are such that generalisations on 'acceptable' traffic volumes, which are related to a random flow of vehicles, are meaningless. Traffic volumes which are acceptable in streets elsewhere, with similar widths and land use patterns, may be unacceptable in the conditions of Chichester, where the environment has such a special quality that aesthetic considerations must predominate, and the application of standards appropriate to other towns may be positively misleading. It was decided that the most profitable source of study for the conditions of central Chichester and, in particular, the Study Area, was the overall pattern of traffic in the city and its effect in detail, considered in conjunction with pedestrian movements and aesthetic factors, in the main streets and minor streets of the Study Area. Surveys of vehicular and pedestrian movements were, therefore, undertaken* (4.34), the material from which supplemented, in greater detail, the information already available from the surveys carried out in 1962, before the preparation of the Reviewed Development Plan (4.02). Although closure of the main streets to traffic is proposed (4.14), pedestrian delays were measured, according to Professor Buchanan's suggested method, as it was felt that this information would be of some value for comparison with busy shopping streets in other towns, and also for reassessing the justification for the traffic proposals in the Reviewed Development Plan. The material from these surveys was considered in conjunction with the appreciation of the environmental areas already carried out.

6.99 Studies involving the measurement of noise and fumes were not carried out, as it was felt that the value of the results in the relatively small scale environment of Chichester would not have justified the expense. It was considered that the effects of vibration, although likely to accelerate damage caused initially by neglect or by the demolition of adjacent buildings (6.61), were not so serious as to justify an individual study. The traffic figures supported this assumption.

*See bibliography for vehicular and pedestrian movement in the Chichester Study Area (1967)

Traffic in the main streets

6.100　The flow of traffic in all the four main shopping streets was heavy, being 8,000 to 11,700 passenger car units per twelve-hour day *, with the heaviest flows in East Street. These figures are specially significant in relation to the intensive use made of these streets for shopping. Check counts on pedestrian crossing movements showed that in East Street, for example, the number of pedestrians crossing the stretch of road which is part of the proposed pedestrian precinct was two to three times the total number of vehicles passing along the road, in a fifteen-minute period. Delays to pedestrians crossing East Street averaged about ten seconds.

Traffic in the minor streets

6.101　In the minor streets, traffic flows were considerably less, and in the one-way streets within the Study Area, flows varied from 360 to 750 passenger car units per twelve-hour day. These figures are relatively small, and well below the generally recognised 'acceptable' flow of about 300 passenger car units per hour for residential streets within an environmental area. Nevertheless, the aesthetic quality of these streets and the fact that they are very narrow and, in some places, winding, mean that even a few vehicles are intrusive.

6.102　An examination of the composition of the traffic showed that in North, West and South Pallants, 20 to 60 vehicles per day were commercial vehicles other than light vans (6.85). Of even more significance is the fact that the entry of these vehicles into the area tends to be concentrated at particular times of the day, especially during the morning. On many days, a quarter to a half of the daily total of commercial vehicles pass through within an hour or less. Already the number of large vehicles, especially delivery vehicles which wait in the streets, is remarked upon unfavourably by residents of the Pallants (6.86).

Conclusions

6.103　If the proposals in the Reviewed Development Plan are carried out, the only streets in the Study Area which will remain open to general traffic are minor streets (4.14). There are two inter-related factors which it is necessary to consider; the likely volume of traffic in the area when the proposals are put into effect, and the environmental capacity of the streets which will remain open to vehicles, taking particularly into account the historical and aesthetic factors.

*It is established practice to measure traffic volumes made up of different types of vehicles by one common factor, a passenger car unit, it is therefore necessary to apply a weighting for all vehicles and the following weightings have been adopted:

motor cycles	0.67
cars	1.00
light goods vehicles (30 cwt and under, unladen weight)	1.00
heavy goods vehicles (over 30 cwt unladen weight)	1.75
buses and coaches	2.25

6.104 Estimates of future traffic volumes for such a small area, where none of the streets will form part of the principal traffic network, cannot be made with accuracy, because of all the variables to be taken into account. Predictions could be seriously wrong if even minor unforeseen changes occur.

6.105 It is difficult to determine environmental capacities of streets such as those in the Study Area, where aesthetic considerations are paramount (6.98). The most appropriate course is to plan for the elimination or substantial reduction in the numbers of extraneous vehicles in these streets, and for the careful control of the future development of traffic generating uses.

6.106 The recent traffic survey showed, even more emphatically than the previous survey, that the present traffic flows in the main streets are quite unacceptable for busy shopping streets with considerable pedestrian movements. The results of the survey amply justify the proposed removal of traffic from most of the main shopping streets. Although the general level of traffic in the minor streets in the Study Area is not, at present, excessive, the configuration and scale of the streets is such that the presence of extraneous commercial traffic and, particularly, waiting vehicles is undesirable (6.86).

6.107 Careful consideration needs to be given to the relationship between future land uses and traffic generation, particularly with regard to servicing and parking. Traffic to and from car parks is an important element in some of the streets (6.82), and should the turnover of cars in the central car parks be high enough to cause excessive traffic in adjoining streets, it will be possible to adjust the frequency of the use of the car parks by means of a pricing policy.

6.108 The patterns of traffic movement and rear servicing proposed in the Reviewed Development Plan will result in great improvement in the quality of the environment in the Study Area. Provided there is appropriate control of land use, the amount of traffic in the streets which are to remain open to general traffic would be likely to remain at an acceptable level.

Summary of environmental appraisal (Key 1)

6.109 The Study Area was selected because it contains three of the distinctive environmental areas which have been indentified in the city centre (5.29).

6.110 The three areas provide very marked and attractive contrasts. First there is South Street (6.05), a busy shopping street, with a fairly high degree of variation in the scale and materials of its buildings, still generally harmonious, and forming a pleasant though not outstanding townscape. Secondly, there is the Pallants (6.11), quiet and unfrequented by comparison (6.78); still partly residential but including a large number of professional offices, and providing a predominantly Georgian architectural character which is surprisingly consistent despite great variety in the detailed designs and scales of individual buildings, most of which are maintained to high standards. In both South Street and the Pallants, the close knit urban quality of buildings which line fairly narrow streets, nearly continuously in most places (6·56), contrasts with the spaciousness of the open area to the south, south-east and east of the Pallants which comprises the third of the environmental areas (6.19).

6.111   The survey also revealed that, between and around these areas of distinctive environmental quality, there are areas which have no positive environment character. These include :

(a) The backland between North Pallant and South Street where gardens, former gardens and yards are used for a variety of purposes or, in many cases, not used at all (6.56). This area is framed by back elevations of buildings, some of which are attractive, others unsightly or spoiled by recent accretions (6.43).

(b) The area around the south end of South Pallant and Theatre Lane. The buildings here do not form aesthetically coherent groups, and there are visually unsatisfactory relationships between the buildings, the streets and the adjacent parking area (6.20).

(c) Land north of Cawley Priory, formerly part of the grounds of this house, now disused and separated visually, by trees and walls, from the adjoining spaces (6.19). This is the area which was proposed in the Reviewed Development Plan as an extension to the car park (6.81). It adjoins the ends of large walled gardens of houses in East Pallant.

(d) The area around the eastern end of East Pallant, where there are attractive groups of buildings, the positive effects of which are reduced by the visually featureless spaces, such as the open land east of East Pallant House which is asphalted and used for private car parking (6.14).

6.112   Areas such as these, with little or no positive character, form breaks between the distinctive environmental areas, and so reduce the effects of contrast between them. Even some of the streets which have special urban quality have gaps in their frontages which impair the townscape quality, while the once pleasant landscape of some of the open spaces has been spoiled (6.19). Comparisons with old illustrations and maps (6.03) show how much attractive quality and visual coherence parts of the Study Area have lost. Such quality and coherence could be regained through rearrangement of land uses, through effective control of traffic and by visual enhancement, including the reshaping of spaces, the erection of new buildings to bring back visual definition where it is now lacking, and by improvements to old buildings which have been affected by unsatisfactory alteration.

7 Recommendations

7.01 The proposals in the Reviewed Development Plan and the accompanying Town Centre Map (Chapter 4) form the basis for the course of action recommended for the conservation of the Study Area.

7.02 These proposals are now carried to further stages, following the analysis of the material obtained in the detailed survey of the Study Area (Chapter 6). The Reviewed Development Plan provides the broad framework of dominant land uses in the city centre; recommendations are now made regarding the detailed, complex pattern of uses for individual buildings and spaces in the Study Area. The Town Centre Map outlines the proposed pattern of traffic circulation, vehicular servicing and car parking; refinements and, in certain respects, minor alterations to these proposals are now recommended. In addition, a range of problems relating to the preservation, restoration and adaptation of old buildings, the improvement of visually unsatisfactory buildings and architectural features, and the layout of spaces have been considered and analysed, and recommendations made.

Environmental pattern (Key 2)

7.03 The criteria which should be taken into account in the reshaping of urban environment have been established and analysed in Chapter 5. The environmental pattern of the Study Area (5.29) has been reappraised (6.109), and principles have been laid down regarding environmental capacity in relation to traffic (6.95). Areas which lack environmental coherence have been identified (6.111).

7.04 The aim of the course of action now recommended is to improve the environmental quality of all parts of the Study Area, including those parts where the quality of the environment is already high (but still capable of improvement), as well as those parts which have little or no environmental quality.

7.05 An improved pattern of environmental areas within the Study Area, based on the established pattern, can be achieved. These would comprise:
(a) Part of the city's main shopping centre: This includes South Street and the surroundings of the Cross, with an extension along Theatre Lane (where new shops and offices are recommended).
(b) The Pallants: The present environmental area extended eastwards and westwards over areas where new building would take place and existing small spaces re-designed.
(c) The Open Areas: Four fairly sizeable spaces, of which the largest is the Cawley Priory area adjoining the city wall (re-designed as an amenity open space as well as a parking area), the others being used principally for parking and servicing.

L

7.06 With the establishment of this improved pattern the whole of the Study Area would be divided into distinctive environmental areas, and the effects of immediate contrast between different types of environment would be restored. Such effects are still strongly apparent in certain other parts of the city (as between the cathedral precinct and the immediately adjoining shopping area), but have been lost or reduced in the Study Area because of the existence of many intermediate areas of land which have no positive shape or character (6.112).

Vehicular movements and servicing of properties (Key 4)

Proposals in the Reviewed Development Plan

7.07 The Reviewed Development Plan envisages the exclusion of as much extraneous traffic as possible from the city centre (4.07) so as to ensure the minimum of detriment to the quality of the environment. The proposed primary road network would encircle the city in the form of a ring road, with circulatory traffic systems outside the sites of the city gates (4.09). Some of the existing roads in the central area would form distributor roads, bringing essential traffic into the city centre, and others would become service roads carrying traffic from the distributor roads to servicing areas, car parks or individual properties. The greater part of the shopping centre would become a pedestrian precinct. (4.14).

7.08 The Study Area is bounded by the proposed pedestrian precinct and the cathedral precinct (5.21) on the north and west sides, and by a section of the city wall to the south-east, all of which would form barriers to the passage of traffic in these directions. Vehicular access and exit points to and from the Study Area would therefore be limited to two localities on the south and east sides of the area, connecting with the proposed traffic circulatory system at Southgate (4 10) and with distributor roads at and near to the east end of East Pallant (7.15). North, South, West and East Pallants would, in the Reviewed Development Plan, remain open as service roads for a limited amount of traffic. All would be one-way streets except for North Pallant, which would become a cul-de-sac, and the southern end of South Pallant, which would be open to two way traffic as far as the entrances to the car parks. South Street would remain open, for servicing traffic only, as far north as a point just beyond the entrance to Cooper Street; the remainder of the street would form part of the proposed pedestrian precinct (4.14).

7.09 The Reviewed Development Plan envisages a mini-bus service (4.31), for which a number of alternative routes have been suggested, some of them passing through the Study Area. Provision is made for off-street servicing facilities for as large a proportion of the commercial premises as possible (4.16). The means of servicing proposed for the two main parts of the Study Area are as follows:

The Shopping Area
7.10 In the Reviewed Development Plan a servicing area is proposed on backland (much of which is now little used) behind properties in the angle of East Street and South Street. This would provide off-street servicing for properties in both streets, including some in East Street outside the Study Area, and would be reached by vehicles from South Street through Cooper Street (4.14).

7.11 Other properties on the east side of South Street would be serviced from the existing South Pallant car park (6.82), and by a proposed new servicing road leading north from the car park. Most of the properties on the east side of South Street would then have off-street servicing. Under the Reviewed Development Plan proposals the large supermarket (6.86) would, however, continue to be served, as at present, from West Pallant.

7.12 Properties on the west side of South Street would continue to be served directly from the street (4.14), since off-street servicing could not be provided without serious detriment to the cathedral precinct.

7.13 Properties around the Cross or on the west side of South Street, which would front the proposed pedestrian precinct and which could not be reached from proposed off-street servicing areas, would be serviced by trucking from the south end of the precinct.

The Pallants area

7.14 A few of the residential and business premises in the Pallants area already have off-street servicing access from one or other of the car parks (6.87). More of the properties in the area could be similarly connected to the car parks or proposed servicing areas. The remaining properties in the Pallants would continue to be serviced direct from the streets.

7.15 Access to the car parks and associated servicing areas would continue to be located around the ends of South Pallant and East Pallant (6.82) (including a proposed new link with the East Pallant car park from Friary Lane). It would not therefore be necessary for more than a limited amount of traffic to enter the main part of the Pallants area.

Recommendations following the detailed study (Key 4)

7.16 Traffic movements and servicing facilities in the Study Area have been considered in greater detail, and the traffic proposals in the Reviewed Development Plan are taken to a further stage. Refinements, and alterations in detail, are recommended. Some of the proposed servicing areas will also be used for parking, and this aspect is considered in the next section (7.29). The traffic and servicing proposals are considered under the following headings:
(a) Cooper Street Servicing Area
(b) South Pallant Car Parking and Servicing Area
(c) West End of West Pallant
(d) East and South Pallants
(e) Baffin's Lane Car Parking and Servicing Area
(f) North Pallant
(g) Parking and waiting in the streets
(h) Mini-Buses

Cooper Street servicing area

7.17 In order to provide off-street servicing facilities for a larger number of properties than was envisaged in the Reviewed Development Plan, and to allow waiting and turning space for additional vehicles, an increase in the size of the proposed servicing area (7.10) is recommended, through the acquisition of additional small pieces of land, of which some are under-used and others form parts of gardens. Rear extensions to a few properties, and small outbuildings, would have to be demolished (7.129). Fifteen shops, six offices, a club and fourteen residential properties in the Study Area, together with a

further eleven properties fronting East Street, would be accessible from the enlarged servicing area. A new private forecourt to the south of the restaurant in Cooper Street is envisaged, to replace the existing one which would be taken by the widening of the service road. No public car parking is proposed in the Cooper Street servicing area during the day time or in shop servicing hours (7.48). It would not be possible for all the properties on the east side of the servicing area to have access from the area, and some of these would continue to be served from North Pallant.

South Pallant car parking and servicing area

7.18   Additional properties could be serviced from this area following two relatively small adjustments to the Reviewed Development Plan proposals (7.11). It is recommended that the proposed servicing road leading northwards from the area be widened and extended by acquiring for demolition a small cottage of no architectural merit (fig. 84), small workshops occupied by a dental mechanic and an upholsterer, and largely disused outbuildings (7.70). At the end of the servicing road the provision of a turntable together with a waiting bay is recommended. This will enable the supermarket, which is now serviced from West Pallant (7.11), to be reached from the servicing area. Reference is made in the next section to car parking provision in this area (7.46).

7.19   The extension of this servicing area across West Pallant to the proposed Cooper Street servicing area (thereby simplifying service circulation) was considered but rejected, mainly because of the great cost of acquiring part of or the whole of the supermarket.

7.20   Further extension of the servicing facilities southwards from the South Pallant car park is recommended, in order to provide access to the properties on both sides of Theatre Lane (7.77). Those on the south side would be serviced by trucking across this narrow thoroughfare, which is proposed to be a pedestrian way (7.50).

West end of West Pallant

7.21 In the Reviewed Development Plan it is proposed that West Pallant should remain a one way street from west to east (7.08). This would make it possible for future servicing traffic from South Street to filter through the Pallants to the detriment of the environmental quality of that area. The western section of the street is narrow, and its continued use for traffic, especially heavy servicing traffic, would perpetuate the existing hazards to pedestrians. It is therefore recommended that the west end of West Pallant be closed to traffic, and that the remainder of the street should become a cul-de-sac. This would also necessitate re-examination of the possible mini-bus routes (7.09).

East and South Pallants

7.22 It is recommended that some of the land south and east of these streets, which now form parts of gardens or are derelict, be used to provide off-street servicing for the adjoining properties, in conjunction with the recommended extension to the parking area (7.43).

Baffin's Lane car parking and servicing area

7.23 Further provision could be made for off-street access to properties on the east side of North Pallant, especially if the parking and servicing areas were extended over parts of the existing gardens. It is recommended that land be acquired for this purpose at some time in the future if this is proved to be desirable (7.40).

7.24 It would be necessary for all the properties in East Street (outside the Study Area) which back onto this parking and servicing space to have access to it when the adjoining section of East Street is closed to traffic (4.14). The possibility of constructing a service access from Baffin's Lane car park, at the rear of properties in East Street to the Cooper Street servicing area (7.17) was considered, but rejected because of the high cost of acquiring properties, and also because a notable Georgian building in North Pallant would have to be demolished.

North Pallant

7.25 It would still be necessary for a small amount of traffic to use North Pallant following the closure of the north end of the street (7.08), because it would not be practicable for off-street servicing facilities to be provided for all the properties fronting the street (7.17). The Reviewed Development Plan proposes a turning space at the north end of North Pallant, which would involve the demolition of a shop. It is recommended that, instead, an electrically operated turntable be provided. This would be adequate for the amount of traffic envisaged, and would avoid the necessity for acquisition and demolition of the shop.

Parking and waiting in the streets

7.26 The City Council's policy is that car parking shall eventually be eliminated in the streets of the central area, and this policy is being gradually put into effect. As more off-street servicing access is provided, the need for servicing vehicles to wait in the streets will be reduced, and it is recommended that waiting in streets be restricted to that necessary to serve the properties for which no alternative servicing has been found to be practicable (4.16).

7.27 If all these recommended refinements and minor alterations to the provisions of the Reviewed Development Plan are put into effect, it is considered that acceptable traffic flows through the Pallants would not be exceeded (6.98), although the volumes would be greater at the extremities of East and South Pallants, which would be used by traffic to and from the car parks and servicing areas (7.15).

Mini-buses

7.28 The principle of establishing an electric mini-bus system in the minor streets (4.31) of the central area is accepted. The system would be designed so that the environment is not disrupted (7.21).

Use and design of spaces

Proposals in the Reviewed Development Plan

7.29 The Reviewed Development Plan and associated Town Centre Map provides for the retention of the existing car parking areas in the Study Area, together with a small extension to the Cawley Priory parking area (6.81), making a future provision, within the Study Area, slightly in excess of the present number of parking places. This is in accordance with the Development Plan policy of concentrating future parking provision as much as possible outside the city wall, with no substantial increase in the provision within the wall (4.18). Not all the existing open area adjoining Cawley Priory and East Pallant House would be used for parking, since a small part of the area is proposed, in the Development Plan, to be a public open space.

7.30 The Reviewed Development Plan contains no specific proposals for the detailed treatment of the car parking areas or other spaces, as these were left for consideration at later stages.

Recommendations following the detailed study (Key 6)

7.31 Recommendations are made regarding the detailed layout and visual treatment of the extensive open areas within the Study Area which are used largely for car parking. These aim to improve the environmental quality of these areas as open spaces (7.04), through re-arrangement of the parking places (making provision for approximately the same number of places as was envisaged in the Reviewed Development Plan), in conjunction with new landscaping, improvement in the design and siting of signs and other features, and provision of new pedestrian ways connecting with the Pallants and the shopping centre. Recommendations are also made regarding the visual treatment of these pedestrian ways, of the minor streets, of certain small amenity spaces, and of the streets in the shopping area, including the proposed pedestrian precinct.

7.32 The detailed recommendations are set out under four headings:
(a) Car Parking Areas
(b) Pedestrian Routes and Minor Spaces
(c) South Street
(d) The Pedestrian Precinct

Car parking areas
7.33 Chichester is remarkable for the attractive visual quality of many of its car parks (4.46). In the Study Area, the Baffin's Lane car park (6.20) has been carefully laid out, but is marred by an excessive amount of street furniture and some unsightly rear elevations of buildings to the north; the South Pallant car park is mainly pleasant, because of its small scale and the attractiveness of some of the rear elevations visible from the car park (7.37); but the much larger Cawley Priory and East Pallant car parking area has, in recent years, lost much of the quality it formerly possessed as an open space, although it still retains many splended trees (6.19) (fig 87).

7.34 It is the presence and disposition of trees (4.46) that give many of the spaces in the Study Area much of their pleasantness. Although trees are not, on the whole, conspicuous from the principal streets, they are characteristic of the areas behind the built-up frontages. Trees necessarily restrict the possible capacity of car parks, but they are very valuable in reducing the harsh visual impact of large numbers of parked cars or expanses of unoccupied parking spaces. It would be possible to retain practically every tree in the Study Area if the suggested layouts for the open spaces are put into effect, and it is recommended that new trees be planted at specific points to help create effective compositions in space and colour, and also provide replacements for existing trees when these reach the end of their lives. The emphasis would be on large trees of traditional species which are characteristic of the city, and for which, in the larger open areas, there is plenty of space. The planting of shrubs in many places is also recommended, particularly where they would help to screen parking areas, to define spaces effectively, or to emphasize vistas.

7.35 Large areas of unbroken asphalt surfacing in car parks are inappropriate in the centre of an historic city. Such areas should be visually improved partly through tree planting, so that their apparent scale is suitably reduced. They should also be finished with surfaces suitable to their settings.

7.36 Traffic signs, lighting fixtures and kiosks, are visually intrusive features in some of the car parks within the Study Area (fig. 85). Improvement in the design of traffic signs generally is recommended elsewhere (7.52), and their siting in car parking areas should be effective but unobtrusive. Instead of the usual overall illumination from tall free standing lighting standards, it is considered that more subtle lighting from less obtrusive low level or wall fittings should be used. The entrances and exits to car parks could be improved visually if the free standing kiosk accommodation and gate mechanisms were integrated with adjacent structures (6.19) (fig. 86).

7.37 Many of the car parking, servicing or amenity areas, and some of the pedestrian routes, would be overlooked by the back elevations of buildings which, at present, vary a great deal in appearance. Some are highly attractive, others unsightly (6.43). Improvements to unattractive rear elevations as recommended elsewhere (7.129), especially those which are conspicuous from the open areas, would greatly help to enhance the visual character of these areas.

7.38 Old boundary walls in local materials (3.10), enclosing existing or former gardens, are notable features of Chichester. They often form significant parts of the visual environment of car parks and other spaces in the Study Area, and it is recommended that they be retained wherever possible, either as parts of the boundaries of the spaces or (as at present in some places) as attractive features within the spaces, visually breaking the expanses. Where new walls are built they should be within the limited range of traditional materials.

7.39 The recommendations regarding each of the parking or servicing areas are as follows:

Baffin's Lane car parking and servicing area
7.40 Little improvement is needed here, except in respect of signs and kiosks (7.36), and modifications to unsightly back elevations of some of the properties in East Street (outside the Study Area) (7.37). Old boundary walls in and around the car park are important elements and should be retained. Elsewhere (7.23) it is suggested that further

85 *kiosks are visually intrusive features . . . in . . . car parks* (7.36)

86 *kiosk accommodation and gate mechanisms . . integrated with adjacent structures* (7.36)

87 *East Pallant . . . area . . . lost much of the quality it formerly possessed* (7.33)

88 *shrubs . . . screening the proposed small parking units . . .* (7.42)

89 *an unsatisfactory relationship between spaces and buildings* (7.45)

90 *new building . . . to give greater . . . definition between spaces and . . . buildings* (7.45)

land on the western side could be added in order to improve servicing facilities to adjacent buildings or provide garages for residential properties as the need arises.

Cawley Priory and East Pallant parking area

7.41   A new layout is recommended for this area (6.19), making provision for approximately the same number of parking places as are envisaged in the Reviewed Development Plan (7.29), but greatly increasing the attractiveness of the area as an amenity open space. The replacement of unbroken stretches of asphalt by a variety of finishes in smaller units would help to reduce the apparent scale of the parking area in a manner appropriate to the environment (7.35).

7.42   It is intended that the detailed layout of this area should restore the park-like quality still suggested by the existing mature trees (7.33). The layout provides for a continuous wide grassed strip, extending in a broad arc from the south end of South Pallant to the east end of East Pallant, roughly parallel with the line of the adjoining city wall. A footpath would run along the grassed area, and another along the top of the wall (which is at present inaccessible); there would also be a new pedestrian connection with South Pallant. Trees would be planted to reinforce the established pattern and to anticipate replacement of ageing or diseased trees (7.34). The planting of dense evergreen shrubs would be designed specifically to reduce the apparent extent of the car park by screening the small parking units which form the basis of the recommended parking system (fig. 88). Their grouping along the pedestrian route is also designed to give emphasis to the direction of pedestrian flow and to provide further definition to the spaces.

7.43   An extension of the car parking area over land to the north of Cawley Priory is already proposed (6.81), and further extension is now recommended over parts of private gardens behind East and South Pallants. This land, which is largely separated from the existing area by walls and planting, would be mainly used for parking at a high density; but access would also be provided for servicing the adjoining properties in East and South Pallants (7.22). Part of the parking provision on this additional land would compensate for the loss of private parking places on the land adjoining East Pallant House, on which it is recommended elsewhere that buildings be erected (7.83). The private parking area could be used by the public outside office hours. Retention of the existing walls and trees, augmented where appropriate by the erection of new walls in sympathetic materials, as well as planting, would ensure that the area of intensive parking is concealed from the main part of the area, which, with its parking places carefully integrated with the landscape, would become a pleasant amenity space of positive value to the city (7.31).

7.44   Access and egress arrangements for the Cawley Priory and East Pallant area would remain as at present (7.15), except for the new entrance point from Friary Lane which is proposed in the Reviewed Development Plan. In the recommended layout, the area is treated as a single unit, but there are several places where a barrier could be placed across the vehicular route if it were desired to regulate the volumes and flows of traffic at specific times.

7.45   It is recommended elsewhere (7.93) that a new building be erected on the northern fringe of the area, in order to give greater visual definition to this part of the Study Area, where there is at present an unsatisfactory relationship between spaces and buildings (6.14) (figs. 89 and 90). Parking provision, to serve the occupants of the building, would be made at ground level.

91 *pedestrian routes . . . linking the car parks with the Pallants and the shopping area (7.49)*

92 *old paving stones . . . varied . . . by cobbles or similar materials . . giving a .. .more broken textural effect (7.50)*

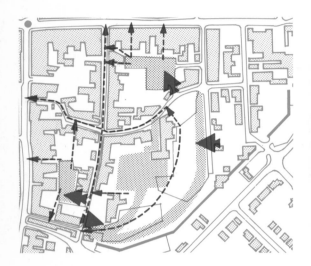

 public car parks

vehicle access points

pedestrian routes from car park to city centre

South Pallant parking and servicing area

7.46   Reference is made in the previous section to the future servicing provision in this area (7.18), including an extension to the south to serve properties on Theatre Lane, and enlargement of the proposed servicing road to the north (7.20). It is recommended that in addition, the area be extended to the east, over parts of gardens and yards to provide additional parking space. This would necessitate the demolition of a mortuary (7.80).

7.47   In order to separate as far as possible the parking and servicing functions of this area, it is recommended that the parking places be concentrated in the centre of the area (providing for the same number of cars as at present), allowing ample provision for servicing vehicles on the western side, and also allowing for off-street access to properties (mainly domestic) to the east and north, together with some new blocks of garages. Trees and old walls already give the northern part of the area a pleasant quality (6.20), but improvements are recommended through further planting, the improved treatment of surfacing, and the better design and siting of signs and lighting fixtures.

Cooper Street servicing area

7.48   This would be primarily a servicing area (7.17), but use for car parking might be possible outside the servicing hours. It would be treated as a utility area, and it is recommended that high walls be erected to give privacy and amenity to the adjoining residential properties, mostly to the east.

Pedestrian routes and minor spaces

7.49   Several new pedestrian routes are envisaged, mainly linking the car parks with the Pallants and the shopping area (fig. 91). Together with existing footways and streets, these would provide a comprehensive and convenient network of routes in the Study Area.

Footways

7.50   Because of their small scale, the visual quality of urban footways depends especially on the textural treatment of adjoining walls and ground surfaces. Old walls of traditional materials in Chichester usually have considerable visual interest (3.10), and special attention would be given to the materials used in new walls which adjoin footways. Old paving stones or setts make a satisfactory and visually interesting walking surface, varied (on the parts of the surface where walking would not actually take place, or would be discouraged) by cobbles or similar materials, giving a different and more broken textural effect (fig. 92). In places the new footways would, as do some existing paths, run through passages in the ground floors of buildings. In determining the direction and form of the new footways, advantage has been taken of opportunities for interesting or even dramatic townscape effects, such as incidental views of notable buildings or spaces through gaps, or the sudden appearance of the cathedral spire as a corner is rounded or a space entered (3.05). Variation in the form of surface treatment of pedestrian routes would be used in order to give direction and to indicate different types of route within the framework of pedestrian movement. Theatre Lane (7.21) would become a pedestrian route, and it is recommended that it be suitably paved.

Existing minor streets

7.51   With the improvement in the system of pedestrian routes, and the concurrent reduction in the number of vehicles as the traffic proposals are put into effect, the Pallants would gradually be transformed into an environment with the emphasis on pedestrian rather than vehicular movement. The parts of North Pallant and West Pallant

nearest to the shopping centre would be closed to traffic (7.21) and would be suitably paved.

7.52 The need for signs and street markings for the regulation of traffic would be greatly reduced. With regard to the general ban on street parking and restrictions on waiting in the central area (7.26), it is suggested that signs be erected at each entrance to the city centre indicating the nature of the restrictions on vehicular movement, supplemented by special signs wherever there were exceptions to the general rules. This would eliminate the need for yellow lines. However, new legislation would be required if these courses were to be carried out. Where statutory traffic signs have to be used, they should be satisfactorily grouped as far as possible. It is suggested that they be reduced from their normal sizes where this would enable them to be better related to the scale and character of the environment, but this again would require new legislation.

7.53 The existing lamp standards in the Pallants are reasonably satisfactory, though some could be improved (6.18). Very special care would be needed in designing new fixtures to replace the existing standards. Consideration would also be given to the visual effects which could be obtained through the highlighting of distinctive features of buildings by the careful placing of lighting fixtures (7.59) (fig. 93). Telephone wires are conspicuous in South Pallant (6.18) (fig. 94) and it is recommended that they be placed underground. If television aerials should become unduly conspicuous, it is recommended that they be centralised to reduce their disruptive effect.

7.54 Small spaces along the frontages to East, South and West Pallants would be filled by new buildings, as recommended elsewhere (7.82), so bringing coherence to the parts of the townscape where these spaces now cause visual disruption (6.17).

7.55 It is not considered appropriate to plant trees along the closely built streets, since they would be out of scale and character, might interfere with underground services, and could reduce the water content of the soil seriously enough to affect the stability of adjacent buildings. Trees in adjoining spaces would be visible in many places from the streets (7.34), either above the buildings or walls, or in places where open landscaped spaces border the streets, as, for example, in front of Cawley Priory.

New small spaces
7.56 The creation of new small spaces of positive character and visual quality is recommended in two places. One is a small piece of land north of All Saints-in-the-Pallant (7.86), now little used but containing some fine trees, which could become an attractive amenity open space accessible from West Pallant. This would help to bring environmental quality to a locality where this is now somewhat lacking (6.111). The other place is behind Pallant House, on the north side of East Pallant (6.12), where the formation of a new paved and planted courtyard is suggested. Other small areas, particularly those associated with shopping or office uses, could be improved in similar ways.

South Street
7.57 As South Street would remain open to servicing vehicles as far as the entrance to Cooper Street (4.14), it would be necessary to retain a carriageway. However, this would be narrower than the present carriageway, with improvement to the pavements, through widening, although it would be necessary to make provision for waiting bays at intervals along the western side (7.63).

7.58 It is recommended that an unobtrusive barrier should be installed at the junction of the pedestrian precinct (7.60) and carriage-way to reinforce the separation, but constructed in such a way as to allow, in exceptional circumstances, a vehicle to pass without damage.

7.59   There would be little need for street signs in South Street, and those that are necessary should be designed to fit appropriately into the environment. It is recommended that the street lighting arrange-ments (6.06) be modified so as to obtain the maximum visual effect from the present disposition of buildings. Some street lamps would continue to be fixed to buildings, as at present, but others would be placed so as to emphasise special architectural and townscape features. Dramatic effects could be achieved by the use of differing intensities of light in appropriate colours and from a variety of sources, thus using to the full the range of lighting techniques available.

The Pedestrian Precinct

7.60   The conversion of existing streets, with their carriageways and pavements, into pedestrian areas or foot streets (4.14) would radically change the character of the environment and give rise to major town-scape problems. These would arise in the proposed pedestrian precinct (7.07), including the northern end of South Street and the other three shopping streets, most of which are outside the Study Area.

7.61   It is suggested that the present streets in the proposed precinct be paved for their whole width, in order to facilitate the passage of pedestrians over the total expanse. This would, however, have the effect of increasing the apparent width of the streets in relation to the buildings (particularly outside the Study Area). The effect could be countered by placing free-standing features at specific points, including showcases, kiosks, public seats or sculpture. Such furniture would be of small urban scale, and sited so as not to disrupt existing important vistas. Opportunities would be taken to use new features to screen existing discordant elements and to create new spatial effects. In some places selected buildings might project in front of the existing building lines, adding interest to the townscapes and narrowing the streets at certain points.

7.62   The actual nature of the ground surface treatment would be a factor of major visual importance. Paving stones or setts would be appropriate, possibly varied in places by cobbles or other traditionally urban materials (7.50). The sizes of the paving units and the nature of the patterns made by the joints would be carefully considered so as to emphasise the essentially urban character of the spaces. Small scale planting and paving in the 'municipal' manner typical of seaside resorts must be avoided completely if the historic county town atmosphere is to be retained.

7.63   Open air cafés would be appropriate in many parts of the pedestrian precinct mainly outside the Study Area. Within the Study Area, there is one place where this type of development would be specially suitable; on the west side of South Street, adjoining the Vicars' Hall, where the pavement would be widened (7.57) and where there are already two established restaurants. Awnings could be erected, together with heating equipment for use when the weather would otherwise inhibit outdoor sitting.

7.64   Advertisements will continue to be strictly controlled by the City and County Councils under the County of West Sussex (Area of Special Control) Order. 1965 (4.48). However, the range of oppor-tunities for advertising would be increased in the pedestrian precinct, and therefore the need for imaginative application of the principles of advertisement control would be all the greater.

Building uses

Proposals in the Reviewed Development Plan

7.65 In the Reviewed Development Plan, the Study Area is divided into three areas of predominant use zoning, corresponding approximately with the three environmental areas (5.29). These are:

(a) South Street and the area around the Cross, forming part of the city's main shopping centre. No extension to the shopping centre is proposed within the Study Area, but provision is made elsewhere in the city centre for the additional shopping facilities (4.26) which it is anticipated will be required as a result of the increase in the population of the the catchment area of the city (4.24).

(b) The Pallants, most of which is zoned for business uses. The sites of the local authority offices (Pallant House and East Pallant House) (6.53) are, however, defined for local government purposes.

(c) The open areas, allocated mainly for car parking, with a small area proposed as a public open space between the Cawley Priory and East Pallant parking areas (6.19).

Recommendations following the detailed study (Key 8)

7.66 It is intended to emphasise or improve the distinct environmental quality of each of these three areas, largely on the basis of the proposed distribution of predominant uses, but allowing for some flexibility where appropriate, and, in the Pallants, placing the emphasis on residential rather than office occupation. Better use of many existing buildings is envisaged, and the erection of new buildings is recommended on sites where they would be appropriate and, in many cases, desirable for visual reasons (7.82). Generally speaking new buildings should be unobtrusive, respecting the scale, proportions, colour and texture of adjoining buildings of distinctive character, and not competing with them in dominance (7.102).

The shopping area

7.67 Most of the shops (6.46) in the Study Area have narrow frontages. Although some are, functionally, reasonably satisfactory, others are in old buildings which have been inadequately converted, are inconvenient in their layout and unsuited to present-day requirements. Upper floors are frequently under-used or disused (6.48) and often in bad condition. Alterations and neglect have sometimes led to instability in the structures (6.64).

7.68 There is a trend, nationally, for shopping units to become larger. However, there are many types of shops which require small premises, and which can flourish especially in the environment of an historical town such as Chichester, with its existing and potential attraction as a tourist centre, its position in a holiday and recreational area and its hinterland with a large proportion of residents in the higher income groups (3.23). Shops of such specialised character would be appropriate in South Street. There are other parts of the city centre where large shops would be more appropriate, such as East Street and the Chapel Street area (4.26).

7.69 No demolition of existing shop premises in South Street is specifically recommended in this report. Planning permission has, however, been granted for the rebuilding of two units near the Cross (7.129), and the possibility of redevelopment elsewhere is not ruled out, provided no buildings of special architectural or historic interest are unnecessarily demolished (7.133) and the new buildings are designed to fit satisfactorily into the townscape. It is recommended that existing shop units in South Street be generally retained, though some combination of adjacent units to form larger shops would be permitted provided that no architectural features are introduced which are out of scale with the street as a whole. The capacity and operational efficiency of many of the shop units could be improved through adaptation of the buildings without adversely affecting their attractive architectural characteristics. Considerable improvements in internal layout would be desirable in many cases, but, when the removal or piercing of partition walls and other structural features is contemplated, care should be taken to ensure that these do not have adverse effects on the structural stability of the buildings (6.68). Improved accesses to upper floors could lead to greater use of these for storage, staff facilities or additional sales space where this would be appropriate (7.71), provided this does not lead to over-loading (6.48) of the structure, or detriment to the external appearance of the buildings through the stored materials being unduly conspicuous from the street (6.43).

7.70 Where the provision of off-street servicing would necessitate land acquisition (6.72) and alterations to buildings, the opportunity should be taken to improve or even demolish existing unsightly or poorly built extensions (7.17).

7.71 Storage and other uses now accommodated in these extensions should in some cases be reallocated within the main buildings on upper floors (6.51), thus releasing the space at ground level for additional sales area and servicing (fig. 95). Sometimes it may be possible to extend shop premises over land at the rear, while in one place (on the west side of the South Pallant car parking and servicing area) (7.18) the provision of a small new workshop over domestic garages is recommended, with access from the servicing area, in order to replace the dental mechanic's workshop which would be demolished in connection with the improvement to the servicing facilities. With the increased use of back land for parking, the rear elevations of buildings (7.129) will become more conspicuous (7.37), and it is therefore recommended that higher standards of design and finishes be established.

7.72 It is recommended that greater use be made of basements (6.47). In their present state they are often suitable for use in connection with certain types of business (as, for example, florists' shops), but with the use of dehumidifiers they could be used for general storage or even for additional sales space, provided structural damage is not caused through the reduction of the humidity (6.74). Where basements are at the present time disused, and no economic use can be found for them, it is recommended that they should not be filled in but be retained as ventilated spaces, to avoid detriment to the structures (6.67). They may prove to be useful if at some future date the premises are used for a different type of business.

7.73 There is considerable scope for the conversion of vacant or little used upper floors into maisonettes or flats. There are many reasons why residential conversions of accommodation over shops have not taken place so far, including lack of financial means or incentive; security and insurance difficulties; the absence of separate accesses to upper floors (6.50); difficulties in conforming to building or fire regulations; and the unsuitability of the environment, as it is at present, for residential uses (6.77).

7.74 Separate accesses to upper floors could often be provided at the rear of buildings. Many of the properties on the west side of South

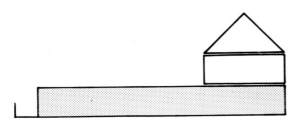

existing use of space

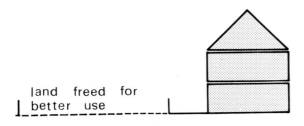

land freed for better use

suggested use of space

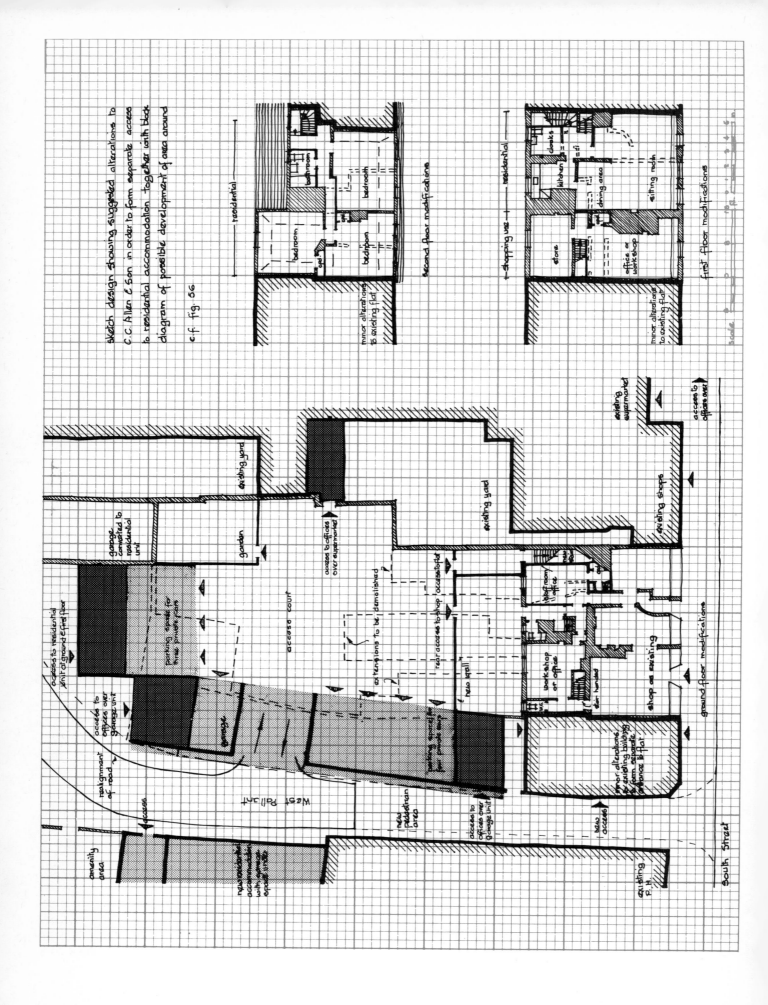

Sketch design showing suggested alterations to C.C. Allen & Son in order to form separate access to residential accommodation together with block diagram of possible development of area around

c.f. fig. 56

second floor modifications

minor alterations to existing flat

bedroom

bedroom

bathroom

← residential →

first floor modifications

minor alterations to existing flat

store

office or workshop

cloaks

kitchen

dining area

sitting room

← shopping use → residential →

garage converted to residential unit

parking space for three private cars

access to residential unit at ground & first floor

access to offices over garage unit

realignment of road

amenity area

residential accommodation with garage space under

West Pallant

new pedestrian area

access court

garage

existing yard

garden

access to offices over supermarket

extensions to be demolished

rear access to shop occasional

existing yard

existing supermarket

access to offices over

existing shops

bed room office

new wall

workshop or office

gas heated

w.c.

shop as existing

access to offices over garage unit

new access

existing P.H.

minor alterations to existing building to form separate entrance to flat

ground floor modifications

South Street

Scale

second floor modifications

96 *separate accesses to upper floors could often be provided at the rear of buildings . . . and so increase their attractiveness for . . . residential use (7.74)*

Street can already be approached at the rear from existing footways, and this would also become possible for most of the properties on the east side when off-street servicing facilities are provided. Removal of most of the traffic from South Street, and improvements to some of the open areas to the east would greatly enhance the environmental settings of properties in South Street, and so increase their attractiveness for possible residential use (fig. 96). Because of this, owners or tenants would be encouraged to convert the upper floors for residential use. The strict application of building or fire regulations often presents difficulties in achieving such conversions, but alterations to buildings would continue to be assessed on their merits by the City Council, as at present, with close co-ordination between the building inspector and the planning officer, and building regulations would not always be rigidly applied.

7.75   With improvements to the environmental settings of many of the properties in South Street, it is considered that there would be a demand for this type of accommodation. Some may be occupied by students of the Bishop Otter College (3.32), for whom an estimate of future needs for this type of accommodation has been made.

7.76   Conversions of old premises in South Street into offices have, in the recent past, often been successful, and other conversions of properties to office uses were taking place or were contemplated, at the time of the survey (6.51). Upper floors which are at present disused or under-used may sometimes be suitable for conversion into offices, where residential use would not be practicable (7.74). The provisions of the Offices, Shops and Railway Premises Act, 1963, may give rise to difficulties in the future conversions of old properties to office use, but these can usually be overcome with skill and ingenuity. It is not the present policy of the City Council that parking facilities be provided for buildings converted to new uses in the central area, since general provision will be made elsewhere, particularly outside the city wall (7.29). It would therefore not be necessary to make specific parking provision for converted properties in the central area.

7.77   The erection of a new building on a site on the south side of Theatre Lane, now occupied by sub-standard cottages (6.16) and a funeral director's office, is recommended (7.20). This would have shop units on the ground floor, with about 2,000 square feet of floor space (so providing a small extension to the shopping area which was not envisaged in the Reviewed Development Plan) with offices above. It is envisaged that this building would be similar in general proportions to the existing shop and office building to the west, with which it would group, providing a firm definition to the edge of the inner part of the city over the site of a section of the city wall which has been demolished, and where such definition is at present lacking.

The Pallants
7.78   Nearly all the properties in the Pallants were formerly residential. With a very few exceptions, they are now used, in approximately equal measure, for residential and office purposes (6.52). A high proportion is in reasonably good condition, and there is considerably less disused accommodation on upper floors than in South Street.

7.79   It is recommended that, in future, emphasis be placed on maintaining and enhancing the character of the Pallants as a residential environment. Continuation of established office uses would be acceptable, but it is recommended that there be no further conversions of existing residential accommodation to offices, except in special circumstances. Of the three properties in the Pallants which were vacant at the time of survey (6.52), two (in East Pallant and West

97 *the present gap in the street frontage is specially noticeable* (7.84)

98 *a new building . . . following the former frontage line* (7.84)

Pallant) were the subject of planning permissions for conversion into offices. As West Pallant now contains only a relatively few premises still in residential use, it would be desirable if the vacant property there were to remain residential, but a compromise might be acceptable with offices on the ground floor and flats above. East Pallant would, however, contain a substantial proportion of residential accommodation if development recommended in this report (7.83) were carried out, so that the establishment of an additional office use in the vacant property there would be acceptable. Some adaptations to existing office premises would be appropriate, particularly in order to comply with the Offices, Shops and Railway Premises Act, 1963 (7.76). One sizeable vacant Georgian house in North Pallant would need fairly substantial alteration for a satisfactory conversion to be achieved.

7.80   One of the few buildings in the Pallants area which are not in office or residential use is a former furniture warehouse in South Pallant, in respect of which there was an application for planning permission at the time of survey for conversion into a Masonic Hall. This building may be extended over land at the rear, and reference is made elsewhere to suggested alterations to the façade which would improve its external appearance (7.128). An existing mortuary would be affected by the enlargement of the car park (7.46), and this could be replaced by a new building on a site adjoining the existing funeral director's offices and garages.

7.81   It is recommended that more intensive use be made of All-Saints-in-the-Pallant (6.26), where a service is now held only once a year. Use for cultural and social purposes would be desirable. However, it is understood that effective steps are being taken to find suitable uses for the church, and that it might well become the duty of the Redundant Churches Fund (financed partly by the Government, partly by the Church Commissioners and partly by the sale of sites) to preserve it.

7.82   The survey revealed that there are many pieces of open land within or on the fringe of the Pallants which, in their present condition, detract from the environmental quality of the area as a whole (6.17). Improvement of two of these as minor open spaces has been recommended elsewhere (7.56). Most of the remainder are suitable for the erection of new buildings which, if well designed in relation to their surroundings (7.66), could greatly improve the visual quality and cohesion of the area. It is recommended that buildings be erected on the following sites, to be used for residential or office purposes as indicated:

East Pallant, east end
7.83   Five new residential units are suggested on the land now used for private car parking east of East Pallant House, re-creating the continuous street frontage which formerly existed (6.14). New parking provision would be made on nearby land in compensation (7.43).

East Pallant, north side
7.84   Here, the present gap in the street frontage is specially noticeable (6.14). A new building is suggested for this site, containing office accommodation with two flats over, and following the former frontage line (figs. 97 and 98). On a vacant site further to the east, the erection of two residential units, one two-storeyed and the other single-storeyed, is recommended. These would be sited so as not to obscure the existing view of the cathedral spire at this point.

West Pallant, west end
7.85   New office and residential accommodation along the curving

99 *part . . . which lacks coherence* (7.85)

100 *new . . . accommodation . . . defines clearly . . . the street* (7.85)

frontage south-west of All Saints Church (6.12) is suggested (figs. 99 and 100). This would not only define clearly a part of the street which lacks coherence, but would largely conceal the back of the supermarket which is such an inappropriate feature in West Pallant (7.126). The existing barn would be retained and restored as part of the new group of buildings (figs. 101 and 102).

7.86 A small extension to the public house on the north side, containing residential accommodation over garaging space, is suggested. This would hide the present unattractive view of the backs of the premises fronting onto South Street and would reduce the wide gap between the public house and the church (figs. 103 and 104). This building would group with All Saints Church, and the recommended small amenity open space on the adjoining site (7.56).

7.87 With the west end of West Pallant built up in this way, there would be an effective visual transition between the environment of South Street and that of the Pallants, at the point where the townscape is dominated by All Saints Church.

South Pallant, west side
7.88 It is recommended that most of the existing gaps (6.15) be filled with new residential units. Six new units are suggested, designed to conform with the existing small scale of the street, but leaving space for an adequate entry to the South Pallant car parking and servicing area. The suggested new buildings at the entrance to the car park would follow the general building line as far as is consistent with safe vehicular access. By building flats at first floor level, with parking space underneath immediately adjoining the entrance, both good visibility and a continuous visual effect from the street would be provided. Part of the land which is recommended for this development is now used for private parking, but alternative provision would be made for this at the rear of the properties, with access from the car park (7.47).

South Pallant, east side
7.89 It is suggested that the obsolescent garage block (which would be replaced by new accommodation elsewhere) to the north of the entrance to Cawley Priory be replaced by a terrace of four new dwellings, providing an effective terminal feature to the continuous townscape on this side of the street (6.15) (figs. 105 and 106). Because of the narrowness of the street at this point, it is suggested that the pavement be set back behind arcading to the ground floor of the new building, with the upper floors brought forward to the existing building line. Reference is made elsewhere to the suggested alterations to the neighbouring warehouse (7.80).

Garages and accesses
7.90 Each new unit would be provided with a garage. It is recommended that no vehicular access from individual domestic properties in the Pallants should open directly on to the streets, but that single access points be provided to serve groups of properties.

The open areas
7.91 Details of the recommended layout of these areas are outlined in the previous section of this chapter (7.33). The erection of new buildings is recommended on the following sites on the fringes of the Cawley Priory and East Pallant parking area.

Adjoining Cawley Priory
7.92 A small office block to the north of Cawley Priory is recommended, which would group well with the existing former house (6.19) and with the possible future extension of the buildings to the north which may be used as a Masonic Hall (7.128).

101 *the back of the supermarket . . . an inappropriate feature* (7.85)

102 *the existing barn would be retained and restored as part of the new group of buildings* (7.85)

132

103 *the present unattractive view of the backs of the premises on . . . South Street (7.86)*

104 *would hide the . . .view . . . and reduce the wide gap (7.86)*

105   *the obsolescent garage block* (7.89)

106   *replaced by a terrace of four new dwellings,
providing an effective terminal feature* (7.89)

7.93   A fairly large office block on the edge of the existing car parking area to the east of East Pallant House (6.19) is recommended. This would have an open ground storey to be used for parking (7.45) and would be similar in general scale to the old main façade of the house, with which it would group architecturally, providing definition to the adjoining spaces. It could also form a significant feature in the south-ward view along Baffin's Lane. Elsewhere it is recommended that the open land to the north, now a private car parking area, be used for the erection of new housing fronting East Pallant (7.83).

Restorations and alterations (Key 10)

7.94   The Study Area contains a high proportion of buildings which are of earlier than Victorian date (6.25). Although many of these, especially in the shopping area, are in bad condition or have been altered detrimentally, others, particularly in the Pallants, are well maintained and have retained their attractive historical character.

7.95   Because the visual character of much of the Study Area is very attractive, buildings, or parts of buildings, which are badly designed, or seriously out of character with their environment, seem specially intrusive.

7.96   Recommendations are now made indicating effective means by which the restoration of old buildings and their suitable adaptation for present and new uses may be secured, and the appearance of buildings which have been badly altered, or which are basically unattractive, may be improved. If these recommendations are put into effect, it will not be necessary, in the Study Area, for any old or historic building of significant architectural or historical interest to be demolished.

7.97   The recommendations are set out under the following headings :
(a) Repairs and adaptations
(b) Improvements to the external appearance of buildings
(c) Improvements to architecturally intrusive buildings
(d) Improvements to rear elevations

Repairs and adaptations

7.98   The Survey has revealed the serious extent of disrepair and structural instability in many buildings in the Study Area, particularly in South Street (6.63). Structural instability in old buildings is often due to alterations having been carried out without proper under-standing of the nature of their structures (6.75).

7.99   Alterations to buildings which may be desirable or necessary in order to secure more efficient use of shop premises (7.69), or in order to adapt upper floors to new uses (7.73), must be carried out with sympathetic understanding and knowledge of the effects of such alterations on the structure and appearance of old buildings. The restoration of old buildings, and their adaptation for new uses or to meet modern standards is a specialised activity and requires con-siderable knowledge of the nature and form of old buildings generally. Knowledge of the types of old buildings which are specially charac-teristic of particular areas is also necessary ; in Chichester the fact that so many buildings are internally timber framed but externally of brick (6.33), and that many walls below ground level are less substantial than they look at first sight, lacking proper foundations (6.34), are important considerations which need to be taken into account.

Architects, surveyors, and craftsmen with specialised knowledge relating to old buildings can, using imagination, ingenuity and skill, put into sound order old buildings which have fallen into serious disrepair, or adapt them for new uses or to meet new requirements, while preserving, or even enhancing their attractive architectural character. However, this may sometimes require relaxation of the strict application of the building regulations (7.74).

7.100   Old buildings need to be regularly inspected. Maintaining buildings continually in good order, with faults put right as they occur, is usually far less costly than carrying out substantial repairs after long periods of neglect. It is considered that the better use of upper floors which are now disused or not put to intensive use (6.65) would ensure that they are kept in reasonable repair.

7.101   Certain old and notable buildings are in imminent need of repair work. The Dean and Chapter (4.43) are carrying out a study of the range of properties in their ownership on the west side of South Street and originally forming part of the Vicars' Close (6.08), in order to establish the cost of the work which would be necessary to adapt these premises satisfactorily for present and future uses, and preserve their attractive character. Some of these buildings are in good repair, but others are in poor structural condition. Two other notable buildings in the Study Area for which repair work is recommended in the immediate future are a former granary behind premises in South Street (6.29) for use for private functions or as a showroom, and a barn in West Pallant (7.85). The latter is important mainly for townscape reasons.

7.102 Problems often arise as to the style in which new additions or alterations to old and attractive buildings should be designed. Where the extent of the new work is fairly small in relation to the old work which is to be retained, it is often desirable that the new work should be in the original style and in materials similar to, or harmonious with, those existing. Where substantial additions and alterations are made, it would generally be more appropriate to build to a new design, offering contrast to the older portions (where they remain visible) or with neighbouring buildings, provided that the scale of the old building is retained (7.66). Reference is made elsewhere (7.111) to the problems relating to the design of new features such as shop fronts in old buildings.

7.103 When old buildings are altered, it is important to consider the effect of the roof line. Roof lines in the city are full of minor variations (3.09), and chimneys, dormer windows, eaves and cornices as well as gables, roof slopes and ridges all contribute to the variety. It is important to preserve the effect of infinite small-scale variety, and the loss or detrimental alteration of features which contribute to this effect would be resisted.

7.104 Many buildings retain attractive and interesting internal features, such as staircases, panelling, ceilings or fireplaces (fig. 107). It is recommended that notable features such as these be retained if possible when buildings are altered or modernised. Where removal is unavoidable it is recommended that such features be preserved, if possible, for re-use elsewhere (7.124). In some cases, it is possible to preserve attractive exteriors while interiors are entirely reconstructed; a building where this was being done at the time of survey is Flint House in South Street (6.31).

7.105 Problems sometimes occur regarding large rooms in substantial old houses, which may be too spacious for modern needs. Some rooms which are excessively high could be modified by the introduction of intermediate floors over parts of the space, without cutting across windows, thus giving added floor area without detracting from the proportions. Occasionally, two existing storeys might be replaced by three within the same space, particularly at the rear of buildings where new patterns of fenestration could be introduced without detriment to the architectural character of the buildings.

Improvements to the external appearance of buildings

7.106 The survey revealed that many of the old buildings in the Study Area are of composite date, and have reached their present form through a series of alterations and adaptations (6.24). Often, however, they have uniform and classically proportioned facades of the Georgian or early Victorian periods. In the shopping area, the insertion of shop fronts has radically changed most of the facades at ground floor level, but many remain largely in their original form above the shops. In the Pallants the majority of the old facades survive largely intact. However, in both areas, the exteriors of some of the buildings have suffered alterations, usually to their detriment, through the removal or mutilation of original features, or the addition of new features. Colours and textures of external surfaces are sometimes inappropriate, while several of the shop fronts are visually unsatisfactory in relation to their settings (6.41).

7.107 In the subsequent paragraphs recommendations are made regarding the reinstatement of old features, the improvement of shop

108 *significant external ... features ... should be restored* (7.108)

109 *would largely regain their original appearance* (7.108)

fronts in old buildings or settings (7.111), problems relating to colour and texture of materials on the exterior of buildings (7.118), and the use of old materials and old features (7.124).

Reinstatement of old features

7.108 It is recommended that significant external architectural features which have been removed or mutilated should in many cases be replaced or restored if buildings would thereby largely regain their original appearance (figs. 108, 109 and 110). These could include mouldings, a door or a window surround, a canopy and brackets, a fanlight over a doorway, a panelled door, a frieze, a cornice, a balcony or railings.

7.109 Many Georgian windows have been altered, to the detriment of the appearance of the buildings as a whole. Glazing bars have often been taken out, and small panes (5.11) replaced by plate glass. Sometimes sashes have been replaced altogether, within the old openings, by windows of different form. Occasionally even the shape of windows in Georgian façades has been altered by widening or partial blocking; an unfortunate example of this is afforded by a house in East Pallant which is very conspicuous in the townscape. It is recommended that, wherever possible, windows in Georgian façades be restored to their original Georgian proportions and appearance (figs. 111 and 112).

111 *occasionally even the shape of windows in Georgian façades has been altered* (7.109)

112 *it is recommended that . . . windows in Georgian façades be restored* (7.109)

Improvements to shop fronts

7.110   A few pleasant nineteenth century shop fronts survive (6.39), but most of the existing shop fronts in the Study Area are of twentieth century date. Only a small proportion are entirely satisfactory visually, in relation to their setting, and some contain features which are seriously intrusive in the street scenes (6.41).

7.111   Plate glass windows need not necessarily be out of keeping with an historical environment, as is demonstrated in the Victorian shop front south-east of the Cross, the new shop north-east of the Cross (6.40), and the recently converted estate agents' premises on the east side of South Street (6.38). In all these, the plate glass windows are greater in height than width, and are separated by stretches of wall or structural features, so that the shop fronts have an overall vertical emphasis and relate well, in scale and disposition, to the rest of the buildings and to the townscapes in which they are set.

7.112   The most intrusive shop windows are those where there are large expanses of plate glass, giving a horizontal emphasis which is at variance with the repeated small scale vertical emphasis of the old buildings in the city streets (5.11). One example is the motor show-room on the west side of South Street (6.46). Here the vertical emphasis could be restored by dividing the elevation into bays of normal shop width through the skilful use of colour and materials, and by varying the shapes of windows (figs. 113 and 114). Where a shop facade has large, ill-proportioned fenestration, reducing the windows to more appropriate size and proportions need present no structural difficulties (figs. 115 and 116). Near the corner of East Street and North Street is a recently built furniture shop with a disproportionately large window. In this case, it is suggested that the shop facade be set back behind an arcaded footway which would link with the covered way of the corner building, thus detracting from the horizontal effect and at the same time forming a distinctive feature in a very important part of the city's townscape (figs. 117 and 118).

7.113   It is recommended that many of the fascias in the shopping area be replaced or improved, often by reduction in depth and by re-setting at lower levels. Where shops now extend over two or more properties the original shop units should be defined by a series of individual fascias, in preference to a continuous unbroken one. In places, lettering could be applied directly to the fabric of the building, to avoid an inappropriate horizontal band of fascia boards.

7.114   The design of lettering in shop names needs special consideration, and there is considerable scope for improvement in this respect in the Study Area. There are some very attractive hanging signs in Chichester and it is recommended that more should be permitted at specific points where they would be most effective visually. Other improvements could be achieved by carefully considered colour schemes, or the use in shop fronts of materials more acceptable in the historic setting. These factors are considered in subsequent paragraphs (7.117).

7.115   It would be desirable to control advertising placed on the insides of shop windows which are conspicuous from the street (6.41). However, this is not possible under existing legislation, and it is recommended that consideration be given to extending the scope of advertisement control (4.48) to cover this form of advertising.

7.116   It is suggested that curtaining be used behind the windows of upper floors which are used for storage, or where tubular light fittings are unduly conspicuous, so as to reduce the detrimental effect from the streets (6.41).

113 *horizontal emphasis which is at variance with the repeated small vertical emphasis of the old buildings (7.112)*

114 *vertical emphasis could be restored by dividing the elevation into bays of normal shop width (7.112)*

115 *a shop facade has large ill proportioned
fenestration* (7.112)

116 *reducing the windows to more appropriate size
and proportions* (7.112)

143

117 *a shop with a disproportionately large window*
(7.112)

118 *set back behind an arcaded footway (7.112)*

Colour and texture of facades

7.117   In the city centre the predominant colours are the reds of local bricks and tiles, set off by the grey limestone of major medieval buildings, and also, in places, by the mottled patterns of flintwork (3.10). No improvements in colour or textural effect can be recommended for buildings in these traditional materials, and the whitening or colour washing of Georgian or earlier brick facades should be discouraged.

7.118   Many old buildings in the city, however, are stuccoed or plastered, bringing pleasant variation into parts of the townscape. Because of the dominance of the local bricks and tiles, it is recommended that rendered buildings should generally be treated in subdued tones, rather than in violent colours which would not harmonise with the traditional materials. Roughcast or pebbledash are not suitable materials for treating facades in the old streets of Chichester, and it is recommended that the old building on a prominent corner site in the Pallants which is faced in this material be refaced with stucco or plaster and painted to an acceptable colour.

7.119   There is no reason why intense colours should not be used on parts of shop fronts. but they should always be dominated by larger quantities of less intense colour which would not compete with the old brickwork of the facades above. In this way the traditional colour and textural pattern would be retained above ground floor level but the shopping frontages would present a visually lively effect appropriate in this type of environment. However, the greatest care would be needed to ensure that the colours chosen for the shop facades make acceptable patterns, producing total effects that are stimulating but not jarring, varied but not visually chaotic, and well considered but not too 'contrived' in feeling.

7.120   In order to emphasise the dominance of the traditional materials (5.12), it is recommended that new buildings should either be in similar materials, or have self-effacing finishes so that they would not distract attention from the older facades (7.66). There is little scope for the introduction of new materials in new or altered buildings, and very careful consideration would be needed to ensure that they either harmonise, or contrast in acceptable ways, with the traditional materials. Because of the nature of their texture, many new materials, if used in conspicuous positions, would be quite incompatible with the character of townscapes where traditional materials dominate.

7.121   Carefully considered colour effects can help to enhance positive features of buildings or townscapes, or can be used to conceal or subdue discordant elements. Some buildings should be treated so as to make them more conspicuous, where this would improve townscape effects (such as, for example, one of the few unaltered Georgian facades in South Street which is almost unnoticed because of its drab decoration). Others might be painted so as to make them less intrusive. The effect of groups of buildings of one style forming single architectural units should be emphasised by treating them all in a similar way, through painting all features such as window frames, and gutters where these exist, in the same colour. Features such as downpipes and lighting boxes (6.41) can be faded into the background through suitable painting. Where arches to windows and doors, on brick fronted buildings, are at present unsuitably emphasised by being painted in contrasting colours. they could be repainted in colours which match the brickwork. In other instances, features such as door or window frames can gain distinction if emphasised through tone or colour contrasts (for example, if they are painted white against a darker background, as in many facades in the Pallants).

119 *the most ill-proportioned individual building in the Study Area* (7.126)

120 *sympathetically detailed façade* (be projected) *above an open arcade* (7.126)

7.122 Some buildings are exceptionally important because of their positions in the townscape, irrespective of their intrinsic architectural merits. Examples of these are the buildings to the north of the Cross, and the building at the narrowing of South Street, north of the Vicars' Hall (6.09). The facades of such buildings need specially careful treatment, particularly where (as in the case of the building in South Street) they have relatively little intrinsic merit.

7.123 Improvements in colour and textural effects on street frontages would, it is envisaged, be carried out under a Civic Trust scheme, following the successful example of the scheme for North Street (4.44).

Retention of old materials and features
7.124 It is recommended that materials from old buildings which are demolished or altered, such as brick, stone, tiles and structural timberwork, be retained and stored in a 'bank' if they are suitable for re-use in restorations or alterations to old buildings elsewhere (7.99). Where distinctive architectural features, such as doorcases, iron balconies or railings, have, unavoidably, to be removed from existing old buildings, it is recommended that they be retained, and re-used in suitable positions in other old buildings which are being restored, often to replace similar features which have been lost. The same is recommended in respect of internal features (7.104).

Improvements to architecturally intrusive buildings

7.125 Ideally, visually intrusive buildings should be replaced, but where this is impracticable, it is recommended that alterations be carried out in order to make them less detrimental to the townscape.

7.126 The most intrusive and ill-proportioned individual building in the Study Area is the supermarket (a former cinema (6.40)), the facade of which is set back a few yards from the established building line of South Street. A suggestion is made that the upper storeys of the building be projected, with a more sympathetically detailed facade, above an open arcade. This would enable the large plate glass window to be retained on the existing frontage to the shop without the present detrimental effect on the townscape (figs. 119 and 120). A well-designed new street frontage in this position, with the distinctive feature of an arcade, would add considerably to the visual character of the street. This would be a relatively large scale alteration, but it would facilitate the more beneficial use (most suitably for offices) of the upper storeys of the building, which are at present only partly used, since the floor space is in excess of supermarket requirements. New accesses to upper floors could be provided in the extension, and also from the servicing area formed by the proposed adjacent development in West Pallant (7.85).

7.127 Recommendations are made elsewhere for the erection of residential and office buildings fronting West Pallant, and backing on to the side and rear elevations of the supermarket (7.85). These would largely, but not completely, hide the back of the supermarket building from West Pallant, and it is also recommended that the effect of the unsightly roofs and side and rear walls be modified by painting the roof in an appropriate colour, and by colour washing the harsh brickwork.

7.128 Another visually intrusive building is a former warehouse on the east side of South Pallant, which is out of proportion with the small scale buildings adjoining and in an unsuitable rustic style with a gabled parapet, incongruous in this setting. The harsh red brick is

121 *a former warehouse . . . out of proportion with the small scale buildings adjoining and in an unsuitable rustic style (7.128)*

122 *reduce its apparent scale and achieve a more urban character, making it less obtrusive in the street scene (7.128)*

also out of character with the colouring of the neighbouring houses. Consideration was being given at the time of survey to the conversion of this building (7.80). It is recommended that the opportunity be taken to alter the facade by removing the gabled parapet, hipping back the roof, inserting windows to a new design more appropriate to the setting, and rendering the greater part of the facade. This would reduce its apparent scale and achieve a more urban character, making it less obtrusive in the street scene (figs. 121 and 122).

Improvements to rear elevations

7.129 The back elevations of some old buildings in Chichester are very attractive, especially where they retain large expanses of tiled roofs, but they have frequently been marred by unsightly recent additions (6.72). Modern buildings, which may have acceptable facades to the streets, are often unsightly at the back (6.43). Almost all rear elevations form part of the visual framework of private or public spaces, and the proposals for more intensive use of much of the land behind the street frontages would make many of them more significant features in the environment (7.37). Opportunities to improve many unsatisfactory rear elevations will occur when alterations are carried out, in connection with the better use of buildings (7.99) and with the provision of off-street servicing access. One block of buildings where the rear facades are especially conspicuous in an important environment is that on the west side of South Street, backing onto the open space adjoining the cathedral (6.56). Recent work on some of the properties in this block has greatly improved the appearance of these facades, and it is recommended that similar work be carried out on the remaining properties, apart from those at the north end which are shortly to be replaced by a new building (7.69).

Listing of historic buildings (Key 12)

7.130 At the time of survey, 105 buildings in the Study Area were listed as of architectural or historic interest under the Town and Country Planning Act, 1962. Of these, 72 were on the statutory list (4 in Grade I and 68 in Grade 2) and 33 on the non-statutory list (Grade 3), (4.38). Many of these buildings were specified as being parts of groups of special townscape value.

7.131 In the detailed survey of properties in the Study Area (6.22), a note was taken of the architectural qualities of the buildings, with a view to re-examining the system of listing and the pattern of listed buildings in the area.

7.132 It is now recommended that the number of listed buildings in the Study Area be increased, to include several not at present listed which are of value as components in the street scenes, and that the scope be widened to include buildings of recent, or fairly recent date. Four revised categories are recommended :
(a) Major historical monuments (5 buildings)
(b) Buildings of considerable intrinsic value (54 buildings)
(c) Buildings of less intrinsic value than those of (b) but of considerable value in their settings (63 buildings)
(d) Buildings which make contributions to street scenes, but which are of little or no intrinsic value (18 buildings)

7.133 It is recommended that those in categories (a), (b) and (c) should be preserved, except in very special circumstances, and, if they are in danger of demolition or injurious alteration, that they be made the subject of Building Preservation Orders, until any change in legislation makes this unnecessary by automatically conferring on to all listed buildings the protection now afforded by a Building Preservation Order. It is envisaged that most of the buildings in category (d) should be preserved. If, however it is found necessary or unavoidable for buildings in this category to be demolished, it is recommended that they be replaced by new buildings which contribute at least as much to the visual quality of the environment.

7.134   The inclusion of a building on the recommended revised list would not necessarily imply that the whole building is of architectural or historical interest. Alterations could be made to many of the buildings on the recommended list without diminishing their value; in many cases such alterations, sensitively carried out, would add to the visual quality and architectural interest of the buildings.

7.135   Buildings not on the recommended list fall mainly into two categories; those which have little or no positive architectural or group value, but which do not detract (except possibly in minor ways) from the character of the environment, and those which are unsightly or intrusive. There would be no objections to the former being demolished, especially if they are replaced by buildings which contribute positively to the environment. The latter ought, desirably, to be replaced (7.125), but, where this is not practicable, major works should be carried out in order to improve their appearance.

7.136   Certain sections of street frontage are considered to be particularly important, because of the visual effects resulting from the alignments and the massing of the buildings, in relation to the townscapes. These include the surroundings of the Cross, those parts of the South Street frontages which are specially conspicuous because of the widening or narrowing of the street, and large parts of the frontages in the Pallants. Not all the buildings on these sections of frontage are of architectural or historical importance, but if any are replaced or substantially altered, it is recommended that the present townscape effects be retained or enhanced by preserving the existing alignments and re-creating (or, if possible, improving) the general effects of the massing (7.126).

7.137   Recommendations are made regarding architectural or structural works in respect of many buildings in the Study Area. Major internal alterations are recommended for 25 buildings (all in the recommended categories (b) and (c), except for one building of no architectural merit for which major works, both internal and external, are proposed in order to improve its appearance), and minor internal alterations for 58 buildings (including 49 in the recommended categories (a), (b) and (c), five in category (d) and four others). Major work to facades is recommended for 21 buildings, of which 12 are in categories (b) and (c), and the rest are buildings of no architectural merit for which visual improvements are recommended.

7.138   On the whole, the internal work would be carried out in order to put the buildings into good repair and/or to adapt them satisfactorily for present or future uses, while the external work would be to achieve an improvement to the appearance of the buildings. Minor external work would often include little more than repainting, together with small improvements to detailed features, and would be carried out as part of street improvement schemes in association with the Civic Trust (7.159).

7.139   Buildings in all recommended categories (7.132) would be eligible for consideration for grants under the Local Authorities (Historic Buildings) Act, 1962 (4.40). It is also recommended that consideration be given to the possibility of providing grants through the Historic Buildings Council under a 'town scheme' for which the co-operation of the Ministry of Housing and Local Government and the local authority is required, each making a 50% contribution.

7.140   There are two national bodies which give advice on the use of buildings threatened with demolition or decay because of disuse, the Historic Buildings Bureau (associated with the Historic Buildings Council) and the Society for the Protection of Ancient Buildings. The Historic Buildings Bureau deals with buildings of special interest, towards the restoration of which the Historic Buildings Council is prepared to consider a grant. The Society for the Protection of Ancient Buildings is interested in all notable buildings which are threatened, and maintains an index both of those seeking notable old houses and of houses threatened with demolition, details of which are circulated to the Society's members or are available on request.

7.141   The County Council has investigated the possibility of encouraging interest in preservation by making wall plaques available to owners of historic buildings. These would merely state that the particular buildings were of historic interest. No scheme on these lines has yet been carried out in the County. It is not considered that such a practice would be desirable in Chichester, where a large number of small plaques on listed buildings would not serve a useful purpose and would be visually unacceptable.

Programming and implementation

7.142   The development proposed in the Reviewed Development Plan is programmed to take place in fourteen stages up to 1986 (4.29). The programming and implementation of the proposals which affect the Study Area, directly or indirectly, are summarised under six headings:
(a) Road proposals
(b) The pedestrian precinct and servicing facilities
(c) Car parking
(d) Shopping provision
(e) Programming of other recommended development
(f) Development by Statutory Authorities

Road proposals

7.143   The proposed ring road pattern (4.09) is based on existing roads, which would be improved in successive stages of the Reviewed Development Plan programme, in conjunction with the construction of the proposed traffic circulatory systems (4.10).

7.144   The road proposals would be carried out in the following stages in the Reviewed Development Plan programme:
Stage 2 Widening of Orchard Street (the north-west section of the ring road).
Stage 3 Traffic circulatory system at Southgate.
Stage 4 Small roundabout at Westgate (as a short-term measure pending the completion of the Westgate circulatory system in Stage 14). New distributory road connecting St. John's Street with Friary Lane, affording a new access to the East Pallant car parking area.
Stage 5 Traffic circulatory system at Northgate.
Stage 6 First stage of circulatory system at Eastgate.
Stage 7 First stage of circulatory system at Westgate.
Stage 8 Second carriageway in Orchard Street (the north-west section of the ring road).

Stages 10, 11 and 12 Second carriageways in Market Avenue, New Park Road and Franklin Place (the south-east and north-east sections of the ring road).

Stage 13 Completion of circulatory system at Eastgate (this might take place in Stage 9, which is an interim measure and is dependent on the financial position at that time).

Stage 14 Completion of circulatory system at Westgate.

The Pedestrian Precinct and servicing facilities

7.145   The formation of the pedestrian precinct (4.14) would take place in the stages of the Reviewed Development Plan as set out below. Each section of the precinct would be formed following the provision of adequate off-street servicing facilities for the properties affected (4.16).

Stage 3   West Street, from the Cross to Tower Street.

Stage 4   East Street, from the Cross to Little London.

Stage 5   North Street, from the Cross to Lion Street.

Stage 6   South Street, from the Cross to Cooper Street. At the same time, the remainder of South Street would be closed to all but servicing traffic.

Stage 7   North Street, further section from Lion Street to Crane Street.

Car parking

7.146   Small extensions in the car parks in the city centre including that at Cawley Priory, are proposed for Stages 1 and 2.

7.147   Further provision for parking outside the city wall is proposed in each successive stage.

Shopping provision

7.148   The proposed new shopping area in Chapel Street (4.21) is programmed in the Reviewed Development Plan for Stage 1. New shopping development in the Hornet area (4.22) would, if required, take place at later stages in the programme.

7.149   Certain parts of the proposed road improvements, which were included in the original Statutory Development Plan (4.01), and have therefore been approved by the Ministers concerned, are being carried out at the time of writing this report, in advance of the proposed programming and before the approval of the Reviewed Development Plan. These include the widening of Orchard Street and the construction of a roundabout at Westgate (programmed for Stages 2 and 4 respectively).

7.150   It is envisaged that all the proposed development directly affecting the Study Area, programmed up to Stage 6, could be implemented within five years after the proposals have been agreed by the Minister. It would be necessary for the servicing area at Cooper Street (7.17) the additional facilities from the Baffin's Lane car park (7.23), as well as off-street servicing for properties north of the Cross, to be completed by Stage 4, in order to provide servicing facilities for properties affected by the proposed closure of East Street to traffic (7.145). The extension of the servicing facilities from the South Pallant car park (7.18) would be completed by Stage 6. It is recommended that the closure of the west end of West Pallant to traffic (7.21) should also be carried out in Stage 6, in conjunction with the introduction of the restriction of traffic in South Street to servicing vehicles.

Programming of other recommended development

7.151   Structural repairs and improvements to existing buildings which are in poor condition, or not satisfactorily used, would take place as soon as funds are available. The present condition of many of the buildings is such that work ought to be undertaken as soon as possible.

7.152   Alterations to buildings in order to allow better use of upper floors would often depend on the provision of off-street servicing access, which would be available within the first few years of the programme period (7.145).

7.153   Major work to facades of buildings to improve their architectural appearance would be phased gradually over the whole of the period of the programme.

7.154   Vacant properties on the market at the time of the survey (7.79), will, it is thought, have been bought and put into good repair by the time of the publication of this report. The costs of the improvements to these properties have been accounted for in Chapter 8.

7.155   The alterations to the South Pallant and Cawley Priory (7.41) car parks, and the provision of the extended amenity areas mainly in the latter, would take place gradually over the period, following the initial provision of extra car parking places proposed in the Reviewed Development Plan.

7.156   Other recommended development (including, notably, new housing and office provision (7.82)) would take place over the period having regard to the availability of the sites, the demand for new accommodation of the types envisaged, and financial circumstances. It is not envisaged that the new office block recommended for the site adjoining East Pallant House (7.93) would be erected before the final stages of the programme period, unless there were a strong commercial demand for such accommodation at an earlier date and other circumstances were favourable.

7.157   It is envisaged that, in any event, a Civic Trust scheme for the improvement of the external appearance of buildings, be carried out in the Study Area (7.138) on similar lines to that already completed in North Street (4.44). Work on the new scheme could take place over a fairly long period; a degree of differing standards of maintenance can give a more pleasing effect than that obtained when whole groups of buildings are at the same stage of fresh decoration or relative dilapidation. This scheme is considered separately from the main programme of improvement and development for the Study Area, and its cost is not accounted for in Chapter 8.

Development by Statutory Authorities

7.158   It is necessary to secure the co-ordination of the provision of the various public services (such as water, gas, electricity and telephone) by statutory authorities at each stage of the programme (4.47).

Further programmes for conservation

7.159   This Study is intended to be the first of a series which will cover the whole of the Conservation Area (which will coincide with the central area (5.01)). The north-east quadrant of the walled city, to the north of the Study Area, is suggested for the next Study, and it is hoped that work on this will be in progress if and when the programme of development recommended for the present Study Area is put into operation. Much of the information obtained in respect of the Study Area will be relevant to other parts of the city, and experience gained. on the present Study should enable the next Study to be carried out with more economy of time.

7.160   Much of the course of action recommended for the Study Area is applicable to other parts of the historic city centre. There are a number of individual properties in other parts of the city on which it would be desirable for work to be carried out in the near future, in advance of detailed conservation programmes for these areas ; it is not likely that these would inhibit the later implementation of comprehensive conservation schemes. In any event, it is recommended that further Civic Trust schemes for the visual improvement of certain streets in the city should be inaugurated in the near future (7.157).

7.161   Conservation principles applicable to other towns, and recommended methods of carrying out similar studies elsewhere, based on experience and material obtained from the present Study, are set out in Chapter 9.

Summary of recommendations (Key 13)

7.162   The recommended development is based on three distinct areas (South Street, The Pallants, the open areas), in each of which the quality of the environment would be enhanced through the rearrangement of uses ; better pedestrian circulation ; reduction and re-routing of traffic ; visual improvements resulting from the enhancement of existing buildings ; the erection of new buildings in suitable places and the improvement in the layout and character of spaces.

8 The financial appraisal

Introduction

8.01   Throughout the Study detailed consideration has been given to the methods to be used in securing the objectives, the cost and effect of doing so in simple monetary terms, how and where within the present law and system of land tenure the burden would fall and what alterations in either might be desirable. To do this it has been necessary to interpret the reaction not only of the people directly affected as owners and occupiers of property but of the property market as a whole.

The valuation process defined

8.02   In order to be explicit it is probably advisable to define the process of valuation. This starts with the need to ascertain the price at which one single interest in land may sell in the open market. This interest can be the freehold in possession or subject to a lease or a tenancy, the leasehold subject to a head lease or a ground lease, or the freehold ground rent. Every property has at least one such interest to value and frequently a combination of two or more. It is possible that two adjoining shops may belong to the same freehold owner yet be let to different tradesmen; alternatively, they may be occupied by one lessee who holds his interest from two separate freeholders. In either of these cases each separate interest must be valued. All financial appraisals start here. Two forms of extension are possible, one in space, the other in time.

8.03   The concept of spatial expansion is simple. Assume there are two saleable interests in one property, the freehold and a lease for 21 years; it is only necessary to value both and add them together to arrive at the cost of acquiring the whole property, freehold with vacant possession. Do this for the adjoining properties in say a terrace of six and one arrives at the total value of the block. Add all the blocks per street and all the streets in the neighbourhood or town and one achieves a capital value for all the property within a chosen territory.

8.04   Extension within the time scale is a more difficult exercise. Property is commonly valued as it exists today. It is possible, within limits, to assess the effect of proposals which, when completed, will alter the factors affecting value; these proposals fall into three broad categories, of which the first two are capable of being measured. Firstly, by a change in the physical constituents of the property by extension, addition or reconstruction; by repairing or demolishing the existing buildings; or by the addition or subtraction of an area of land. Secondly, by the provision of amenities contiguous to a series of properties so that they are all affected in a similar manner, for example by the provision of rear service roads and car parks. Thirdly, by the carrying out of proposals that effect a general alteration in the nature of the environment, for example the closure of main access roads to vehicular traffic and the formation of pedestrian precincts. With wide vision but with little clarity it is possible to anticipate an increase in values over a broad area caused by a general enhancement in the tone, a greater attraction in terms of trade and tourism and an accretion of better standards of commercial, recreational or cultural amenities. Unfortunately this breadth of vision leads to lack of focus and definition, and any attempt to reflect this in simple monetary terms is no more than crystal gazing.

Cost/Benefit Analysis

8.05   The application of the techniques of cost/benefit analysis to the study of the conservation area was considered in detail before any attempt was made at a general economic appraisal of the proposals.

8.06   Cost/benefit analysis, sometimes referred to as the planning balance sheet, has been described as a branch of economic analysis which is used to assist rational decisions, particularly investment decisions, in the public sector where market forces give little guide. It is unquestionably the right course of action, when faced with a large number of relevant variable factors, to analyse, collate and summarise the effect of each. This is an exercise which any prudent man would undertake before forming an opinion; there is, however, a vast difference between the way this may be done where the factors are measurable as against the case where they are intangible. The study of conservation gives rise to a number of considerations of the intangible—architectural merit, aesthetic quality and historic importance are examples.

8.07   Although development of the technique has been continuing for some time, analysis of the kind which has in the past produced a planning balance sheet still shows some weakness in tackling intangibles. It restricts its scope to a relatively small area. It evaluates the effect of, say, local through traffic while at the same time looking at the implications of regional traffic using the same routes; logically, this thinking should be extended to consider the effect of, for example, a new by-pass trunk road. The balance sheet may take into account the fact that a particular town has excellent facilities for the extension of its industrial estate but makes no concession to governmental policies concerning the re-location of industry or other artificial controls of a national character which may affect expansion. In both these cases, the effects, either by way of benefit or injury, are difficult to assess and are usually ignored.

8.08   Secondly, the detail of study varies according to the capability of measurement. Construction costs can be estimated with considerable accuracy by engineers and property acquisition or realisation for development can be valued within narrow limits. Against these precise measurements are set the benefits of a particular proposal to the public at large and these are of necessity approximations since they are difficult to quantify in any terms.

8.09   This highlights the main disadvantage of the technique, the lack of a base unit. If a factor is to be considered at all it must be capable of being measured – once measured, it must be set up against one simple yardstick. One can accept that the yardstick of the property market as a whole cannot be used because the market does not react to intangible factors: indeed great skill is required in assessing the likely market reaction to positive proposals which actually touch and affect in a physical manner one legal interest in one property. If a proposal to alter, repair, adapt or improve is capable of description and definition and its completion can be effected within the fairly near future, then it is possible to assess its effect in money upon a single interest in land. The interest can be valued 'before' and 'after'. The result is still opinion, but it is an opinion based upon facts and a careful assessment of the market reaction.

8.10 To carry the principle further into the consideration of the implications of a programme of conservation would seem to take it beyond the scope of informed opinion into the realms of supposition. The analyst tries to balance the costs and benefits of a particular scheme against each other by a system of weighting. His method and reasons for doing so are also his informed opinion but because he has no yardstick of a similar nature to the reaction of the property market, this weighting must necessarily be an arbitrary subjective decision. Until the technique can demonstrate its ability to balance 'poor architecture' against 'great historic importance' or 'cultural amenity' against cost, it will be of little or no assistance in the consideration of a policy of conservation.

Method used in study

8.11 As described elsewhere, nearly every property in the detailed Study Area has been surveyed and annotated sketches produced of the accommodation on each floor. From these surveys floor areas were calculated and information about rating assessments was added together with any evidence that could be gleaned of market value from known transactions in the previous couple of years. The answers given by occupiers as to the terms of existing leasehold interests tended to be incomplete and some difficulty was experienced in deciding which properties contained leasehold interests capable of being valued. Much of the information about leasehold interests is already available to the Inland Revenue Valuation Office following service of their Section 82 Notice under the General Rate Act, 1967 or similar earlier enactments, but, of course, these returns are confidential and could not be made available. Valuations were then made of each individual freehold interest and each separate leasehold interest and schedules prepared. From these flowed totals in respect of each heading used, which have been numbered for cross reference in the Tables.

8.12 One or two general points about the figures need explaining. For example, it is emphasised that 'before and after' values have only been introduced for those properties physically touched by proposals. The net addition in Table I could have been ascertained without putting values on properties not affected since these, being the same 'before' and 'after', balance each other out. First, it was found that an early assessment of all present values was helpful in consultation; frequently the decision to recommend a certain course of action was not taken until the financial consequences were known and it was not desirable to delay the work until there was certainty about which properties were to be touched and which not. Secondly, looking at the overall capital value, and comparing it with total costs and total increase in values helped to give perspective and scale to the exercise. It also gave rise to a certain amount of allied data which, though not specifically used in this Study, may be useful for comparative purposes. All the figures, whether used in Tables or otherwise, are collected in the Summary of Statistics at the end of the chapter.

8.13 With regard to Statistics Item (1), except where a valuable leasehold interest was known to exist, the premises were valued as with vacant possession. It is true that with commercial properties the

Table I
Before and after theory

Present capital value of all freehold interests in Study Area	(1)			3,615,020
Present capital value of all leasehold interests in Study Area	(2)			205,550
Total value *before* **proposed works**				**£3,820,570**
Enhancement in value of all interests affected by communal works	(3)		10,450	
Enhancement in value of all interests affected by individual works	(4)		82,100	
Release of Development Value inherent in bare land	(5)		172,250	
			£264,800	
Deduct:				
Injury to value of all interests affected by communal works	(6)	26,700		
Injury to value of all interests affected by individual works	(7)	46,750		
		£73,450	73,450	
			£191,350	191,350
Total value *after* **proposed works**				**£4,011,920**

Note 1 Difference in value=an enhancement of £191,350.
Note 2 Cost of works, not included in this exercise,
totals £225,510 (Statistics 8 and 9).

effect of Part II of the Landlord and Tenant Act, 1954, may preclude the owner from obtaining possession but it has been assumed that renewal of leases will be at rack rents and that investment value and vacant possession value of commercial premises are not far apart. One or two of the residential properties may be let on statutory or regulated tenancies but the numbers are few and the effect upon the total so insignificant as to allow it to be ignored.

8.14 For reasons which are set out in detail later, the cost of the proposals has been divided into the two measurable categories described in 8.04. One category embraces proposed works which touch and affect a series of properties simultaneously — as for instance a communal rear service road. The cost of these works is shown at Statistics Item (8) where they are referred to as communal works and the effect on values is shown at (3) and (6). The other category refers to work proposed to be carried out on individual buildings or properties — as for instance the re-styling of an elevation or conversion to other uses. The cost of these works is shown at Statistics Item (9) and described as individual works while the effect on values is shown at (4) and (7).

8.15 Trade disturbance Statistics Item (13) has been taken out separately because this is an expense which will only occur if powers of compulsory acquisition are invoked. There is a good case for suggesting that wholesale compulsory purchase is not the right way to implement a programme of conservation.

8.16 Injury can be caused to property by compulsory purchase in two ways, by taking away part of the land or building and also by damaging the value of what is left behind. The butcher's shop example used later on (8.25) illustrates injury by taking part of the building away and how the damage may be aggravated by reducing the value of the remainder even further, by limiting the market. There are occasions when public works, instead of damaging property, cause some enhancement in value. This is usually referred to as betterment and the provision of rear vehicular access where none was previously possible is a case in point. The principles for assessing injury or betterment are the same but while the law of compensation for injury is well established there is no statutory provision for the collection of betterment as such. Where it arises from the action of a public authority the benefit goes to the individual property owner. It is only in cases where both occur to the same property that betterment can revert to the implementing authority by being 'set-off' against injury.

Before and after theory

8.17 Consideration of the overall effect of the study proposals has been limited to the incidence of change in property values between what is apparent today (before) and what can reasonably be foreseen in measurable terms (after). The relevant figures are set out in Table I.

8.18 It must be emphasised that Table I is a theoretical exercise only. No single person is assumed to own all the freeholds; the enhancement or injury to value caused by the implementation of the proposals outlined in Chapter 7 is enjoyed or suffered by the various parties actually affected; and the benefit of the released Development Value goes into the pockets of the fortunate owners of the sites, less the 40% levy. The table is an indication of the overall effect of the proposals in terms of property as a national asset and it is interesting to note that the net increase in value of £191,350 is almost exactly 5% of the capital value of the properties affected, taken as a whole. Against this must be set the £225,510 cost of carrying out the proposals.

8.19 Further tables appear throughout this chapter; in each case the figures used are referenced by a number in brackets, thus (1) to a summary of Statistics at the end of the Chapter.

8.20 Any practicing valuer will be surprised at the apparent accuracy of the figures shown in the various tables. The normal practice of rounding out was avoided for two reasons. First, some of the items are so small that rounding out would distort the proportions and, secondly, a great deal of addition and subtraction of individual values was involved. To use approximations or bring in an end item of 'contingencies' would have made the task of cross-checking and balancing quite impossible.

8.21 Attention must be drawn to the point that no regard has been had to the costs of preparing detailed plans, nor is any sum included for legal or professional fees nor for the costs of administration and implementation. Until a decision has been made as to the method of implementing the proposals which have been considered, it is quite impossible to quantify these initial costs but there seems to be little doubt that in relation to the other expenditure, they could amount to a substantial sum. Furthermore, there is the point that the Conservation Study and detailed consideration of a particular portion of the city all flow from the presentation of the Review of the Development Plan, together with the Town Centre Map. Chichester has been fortunate in having, prior to the Conservation Study, a Town Map framework which seems generally acceptable and lays down quite firmly the way in which the city will progress from the point of view of highway and planning proposals. Had this framework not been available, it would have been necessary to commence the Conservation Study with a consideration of a large number of matters more germane to the Town Map as a whole than to the limited areas of the Conservation Study.

8.22 As indicated earlier no attempt has been made in arriving at the 'after' valuations to include enhanced value in properties not physically affected by the positive proposals; nor, of course, has any account been taken of possible depreciation in property values either within or without the detailed Study Area. It is probable that many interests, although not directly affected, would feel repercussions from the changed environment created in the detailed Study Area. This part of the study has been considered as essentially a practical valuation exercise. Until the market reacts one way or another the measure of these repercussions is sheer guesswork and can have no part in the financial appraisal.

The present situation

8.23 It was apparent from a very early stage of the Study that there seemed ample opportunity for alterations to existing property which ought to result in more beneficial occupation and, at the same time, there was room for development of some small pieces of back land or blank frontage to the existing streets. These aspects were considered at some length in an attempt to find out why the property market has not already taken advantage of the opportunities.

8.24 One reason is undoubtedly that the property market and the structure which serves it tends to be conservative. Thus, novelty by creating pedestrian areas from existing highways is new enough to present particular difficulties in the interpretation of future trading prospects and, consequently, of property values. Traders themselves are divided in opinion upon the consequences which will flow from creation of pedestrian precincts. The advice that a developer receives from his consultant valuer is, therefore, necessarily cautious until time and practice produce results which are capable of clear interpretation.

Economics of upper floor uses

8.25   The point made at 6.66 about upper floors over shops being visually unattractive and poorly maintained when vacant is one which deserves special consideration. Some retailers with shop frontage can do the same amount of business in a single storey corrugated iron building as in a three storey marble-faced emporium. It follows from this that the value lies mainly in 'operational space' and although upper floors may be repaired, converted, adapted or used by a purchaser whose trade requires them, it is not always easy to imagine this space being essential to the functioning of another trade when the present occupier leaves it standing vacant. For every furniture shop which needs spacious upper floor storage, there may be two butchers who do not. If, for example, a shop on three floors becomes vacant and the price asked is £30,000, what is likely to be the demand? If in the market there are two butchers and one furniture dealer, it is likely that the butchers will say that for their businesses the premises are worth only £15,000, whereas the furniture man is quite prepared to pay for the space which he needs and will buy at somewhere very close to the asking price. If the same shop was available with no furniture man in the market it is still only worth £15,000 to the two butchers but they will bid against each other until one of them may succeed in getting the property for £20,000. This reflects the purchaser's estimate of the potential worth in the extra space which he does not want. He anticipates that upon resale, there will be a buyer who wants and is willing to pay for the extra space. In these two imaginary transactions, the two purchasers have probably paid the same price for the ground floor space but because of their different requirements, they have put different values on the upper floors.

8.26   The economics of upper floor use are immediately apparent if one tries to take them away by conversion into a self-contained flat or maisonette. Nobody would attempt to do this to the furniture dealer since he obviously fully uses the accommodation and could even be put out of business by the loss of storage space. What is not quite so obvious though is the butcher's reaction to taking away the upper floors which he does not put to practical use. At first glance, it looks as though the space is worthless but one must remember he paid a good price for it, a price which he expects to recover in the open market upon resale. Compared to the furniture man who paid £15,000 for the upper floors, the butcher has only invested £5,000 but if you take this away from him, convert it, provide a separate access at a cost of, say, £2,500, you still only have a modest flat or maisonette over a butcher's shop in the High Street worth, say, £3,500. Not only have you caused injury to the butcher's interest by taking valuable floor space from him but, by making the property unsuitable except for a trade which does not require the facilities of upper floors, you have restricted the market for what is left.

Fragmentation of legal interests

8.27   Apart from the purely economic discouragement dealt with above, probably the greatest hindrance to the best use of property in the broadest sense, and certainly a major impediment to the retention of a high standard of maintenance, is the fragmentation of legal interests. Frequently the tenure of the property gives no incentive to do anything, either because the tenant has a lease with only a limited period to run, or because the landlord may have some years to wait before the work reflects any benefit to him. It is possible to find adjoining small shop properties subject to separate leases from different freeholders, each shop having accommodation over it capable of exploitation only at economic cost if the two units could be taken together and not treated as separate entities.

Unification of ownership

8.28   Unification of ownership is to some degree the key to much new development and has been the starting point (or the stumbling block) to many projects of town centre development. The problems of tackling any scheme of conservation are different from those which apply to town centre redevelopment and it is not necessarily true to say that unification is either the right answer or the complete answer. It is self-evident that multiplicity of ownership must make the task more difficult since two property owners are more likely to reach identity of views than twenty. Moreover, the fact that property may be in 'public ownership' can itself be a misleading description since there is often just as much inflexibility in terms of property holdings by Authorities as there is in the case of private individuals. The Post Office, the County Library, the Water Undertaking and the Public Car Park are all owned by public authorities but the assets are held in four separate purses guarded by four separate treasurers, each accountable to a different cross section of the community.

Lack of incentives

8.29   A third reason for present lack of action is frequently that the owner, although he may be the owner of sufficient legal interest to do as he wishes with the property and a scheme of improvement could be worked out which is economically viable, may never have given serious consideration to whether the works needed doing. Why should he? If a man's business is as a retail greengrocer is he necessarily going to apply much thought and time to whether the rooms over his shop will be better used for some other purpose than the storage of orange boxes? Or whether he should demolish and redevelop the outbuildings? Or form his own rear service access when loading from the street has served adequately for decades?

8.30   It could be that although there is some benefit in the proposal, this benefit is not a sufficient incentive for the owner to be bothered with all the repercussions. By the time the lawyer has cleared away restrictive covenants, the architect has prepared the plan, obtained planning permission, beaten his way through the Building Regulations and obtained by-law consent, the quantity surveyor has said how much it will cost and the valuer has said what difference it will make to income or capital value and they have all been paid, there may be precious little profit in it. If there is anything the Land Commission may well take 40% and, in any case, the whole project could invite unwelcome attention from public authorities, with more regulations or proposals for an increase in the rating assessment.

Implementation using existing legislation

8.31   A particular difficulty arises where a programme of conservation proposes the carrying out of works to a property that neither increases its capital value nor the income to be obtained. The effects of the works vary according to their nature: straightforward repair will normally add value; some improvements may do the same. Conversion of accommodation may result in a reduction in value which if enforced should be compensated. Thus subsidy may be the financial but not the practical answer. No local authority either has the power to force works upon the owner, to compensate him for any loss or collect any payment from him if the works add value. In the absence of agreement, the authority can only proceed by purchasing the entirety of the property, dispossessing the occupier, doing the work and selling the premises afterwards; the cost of this is shown at Table II.

Table II
Implementation using existing legislation

Cost of acquiring with Vacant Possession all interests in these properties where betterment exceeds injury	(12)			£604,400
Trade disturbance payable to occupiers of above properties	(13)			83,800
Compensation for land taken and injury to other property affected	(6)		£26,700	
Compensation for land taken and injury to other property affected	(7)		46,750	
			£73,450	
Less: Betterment set-off	(10)		5,700	
			£67,750	67,750
Cost of works	(8)	£63,095		
Cost of works	(9)	162,415		
		£225,510		225,510
Total Capital Outlay				**£981,460**
Deduct:				
Assets available for disposal	(12)		604,400	
With benefit of enhancement in value	(3)		10,450	
With benefit of enhancement in value	(4)		82,100	
			£92,550	
Less: Injury set-off	(11)		2,200	
			£90,350	90,350
			£694,750	694,750
Total deficit using the only powers at present available				**£286,710**

Note 1   The 'set-off' items arise because elements of injury and betterment occur simultaneously in ten cases; in six of these, betterment exceeds injury and the property is to be purchased; in the other four, injury is paramount but is offset by betterment to the extent of £5,700.

Note 2   Although not shown here it can be demonstrated that the deficit of £286,710 is apportionable as to communal proposals £101,460 and as to individual proposals £185,250 (see also Table V).

8.32 It will be seen that this method of implementing the proposals achieves the dual purpose of providing statutory power to execute works to individual buildings while ensuring that betterment accrues to the public at large (who are, after all, paying the bill) rather than to the individual property owner.

The need for change

8.33 Further study in depth and major decisions will be required if the Study is to become a reality.
(a) Would amendment of current legislation suffice? or
(b) are new laws required?
(c) by whom and how are the proposals to be implemented?
(d) can incentives be created to avoid the use of public funds?
(e) who is to bear the burden of expenditure and recover any benefit?

Amendment of present legislation

8.34 The scale of expenditure envisaged (nearly a million pounds) leads to the suggestion that the Land Commission might use its funds and powers to achieve wholesale acquisition. Such an approach can only be justified if one accepts that existing legislation must remain undisturbed and that it is right to use the only means available. If it is the only instrument to hand, a steam hammer makes an effective nut cracker but it is a gross mis-use of power. Nobody has yet designed a legislative tool for conservation action but there seems to be little doubt that the presently available procedure could be improved upon. It is cumbersome, wasteful of capital, does not achieve the maximum recoupment possible and involves unnecessary trade disturbance.

Disturbance element

8.35 The disturbance element can be dealt with by a relatively simple change in the law of acquisition and compensation. Specific power is needed to acquire property for recoupment without dispossessing the occupant; a lease-back at current market rental could be the solution.

Development sites

8.36 Secondly, there is the question of the development sites. It is probably true to say that the land suggested for development is not at present suitable for this purpose and will only become so by reason of the programme of works proposed for the whole area. The owners of this land would be prudent to wait until the land is ripe before selling it; when they do so they pay a levy of 40% of the released development value to the Land Commission who have no obligation to use these funds in any particular fashion. The levy benefits neither the present owner of the land nor any other person or organisation whose scheme brought to fruition the release of development value. It would be more logical if the whole of the released value was applied to mitigate the costs of the scheme. Even if the organisation buys the land before implementation of the works, the vendor can insist upon full development value in compensation – so there is no point in doing so.

Implementation using amended existing legislation

8.37   If, however, the implementing organisation could acquire at existing use value, the difference would help pay for the scheme which itself creates the difference in value. The vendor would be denied his profit (which has not been created by his actions) and would, in effect, be paying a 100% levy to the authority instead of 40% to the Land Commission. The difference made by these two relatively minor changes in existing legislation is shown in Table III. Compare the deficit of £59,560 with that shown in Table II of £286,710.

Table III

Implementation using amended existing legislation

Cost of acquiring all interests where betterment exceeds injury	(12)	604,400
Compensation for injury to remainder (as before)		67,750
Cost of all works	(8 & 9)	225,510
Cost of acquiring development sites at existing use value	(14)	28,900
Total capital outlay		**£926,560**
Deduct:		
Assets available for disposal with benefit of enhancement in value (as before)	694,750	
Capital value of land after release of development value	(5)	172,250
	£867,000	867,000
Total deficit by amending present legislation		**£59,560**

New laws required

The three aims to be achieved

8.38 These suggestions do not, of course, strike at the basic deficiency, the lack of properly aimed legislation. Without specially directed power the plan can only be implemented by a public authority wielding the ponderous weapon of wholesale acquisition. What is needed is something less disastrous than compulsory purchase, yet which can achieve three things. First, empower the carrying out of works which appear to be necessary for the successful implementation of a programme of conservation without the need to acquire a legal interest in the property. Secondly, provide for the payment of compensation for any diminution in the value of the property affected, together with the usual clause relating to set-off. Thirdly, provide for the implementing organisation to recover betterment as such.

Implementation using new legislation

8.39 The effect of this is shown in Table IV, although the resultant deficit is unchanged from Table III it will be seen that by proceeding in this manner, the amount of capital to be injected to carry out the proposals is substantially less than by any other means.

Table IV
Implementation using new legislation

Compensation for land taken and injury (as before)				67,750
Cost of works	(8 & 9)			225,510
Total capital outlay				**£293,260**
Deduct:				
Betterment collectible (as before)			90,350	
Release of development value i.e. capital value of land 'after'	(5)	172,250		
Less: existing use value	(14)	28,900		
		£143,350	143,350	
			£233,700	233,700
Total deficit using new legislation				**£59,560**

By whom and how

Trust association implementation explored

8.40   The possibility of using the Land Commission has already been touched upon. Local Authorities might also be the implementing agencies but in any case it is suggested that it might be desirable to provide these bodies with powers different from those currently available. It is open to question whether the right party to implement the proposals is either of these or any other public body. If a group of property owners are persuaded that proposals for consideration are soundly based and properly measured, why should they not be empowered to carry out the projects themselves by, for example, the formulation of Trust Associations? It would follow that there would need to be general powers available rather than it should be necessary for them to resort to Special Acts of Parliament. It may also follow that some power of compulsion may be necessary so that the wishes of the majority may override the unwillingness of the minority. The possibility should be considered of granting the right to acquire compulsorily only a sufficient legal interest in property to enable works to be carried out. There is already a precedent in this in the powers given to certain authorities, for example, Electricity Boards to obtain compulsory easements and to pipe lines companies to acquire wayleaves.

Incentives

8.41   They would need incentives and rules but it is suggested that if, say, 80% of the people affected in any one small area were in agreement, they would be permitted to form a trust and implement proposals overriding any objections received from the other 20%. The trust could be given facilities to borrow capital at a favourable rate of interest if their own finances were not available and they would be required to keep their own accounts. No other incentive would be necessary if within the whole area betterment exceeds injury, because failure to form a trust would force the local authority to act with the possibility that betterment would accrue to the public purse rather than the individuals concerned.

8.42   It should be possible to so define separate areas included in a conservation programme that finances almost balance; by this it is meant that two entirely disconnected areas could be combined so as to permit the formation of one trust. In the first area injury may substantially exceed betterment but in the second area the converse may be the case. If the two are put together, the scheme may have the makings of an economic project. It would encourage individuals to take an interest in their own property and in their immediate neighbour's property, while the question of agreeing values would become far smoother, if the property owners concerned felt that they were combining with their neighbours so as to retain their property interests and defeat the compulsory powers of the outsider.

8.43   Once the scheme had been set up and approved by 80% of property owners affected there would be a very good chance that the proposals may even be effected by the use of private capital instead of public capital and it would also seem that this type of approach would encourage 'conservationists' to look very closely at the economic effect of their proposals.

8.44   The financial consequences are no different from those set out in Table IV — it will be noted that the result is a deficit.

Grants in aid

8.45 It will be obvious that any deficit must be made good from sources outside the Trusts but over and above this there must be, not only a reimbursement of the administrative costs which could be substantial, but also an incentive bonus for distribution amongst the participants. No property owner is going to be troubled by the suggested works if, at the end of the day, he merely breaks even. There must be some incentive or profit motive to repay him for the effort.

Rating adjustments considered

8.46 Some consideration has been given to whether sufficient incentive could be created by manipulation of rating assessments, rate poundage or the further deferment of rating re-valuation. For example rating assessments or the rate poundage might be reduced; alternatively, re-valuation of the property for rating purposes might be at longer intervals than the current provision of five years which at least is currently the theory though not the practice. However it is doubtful whether these measures alone would be sufficient to encourage action.

8.47 It is interesting to note that the total of Gross Values for rating purposes (£77,944) is little more than a quarter of the estimated rental values (£278,404). While accepting that the bases for the two valuations may not be identical, the margin is sufficiently wide to cause some surprise. There are several reasons for it — the time lag since 1962/63 when the last re-valuation was done and the fact that office rents have soared from 7s. 0d. to 20s. 0d. per foot per annum over the last five years must be among the considerations. It is also worthy of note that fashionable cottages in the Pallants commonly selling at around £10,000 have a Gross Value of around £185 only. It could be inferred that the same considerations apply elsewhere in the country, creating similar differentials but no evidence has been collected other than that involved in the study.

Special rate

8.48 Provision might be made for a special rate on the lines indicated in Appendix A. It seems doubtful whether the income produced would be great bearing in mind collection costs, but, if allied to the collection of the general rate, it may well be possible. The scheme is worthy of future consideration, not having been studied in depth as yet, although it should be noted for comparison purposes that the product of a penny rate in the whole of the detailed study area is £250 per annum.

Where the burden may fall

8.49 It was felt that some attempt should be made to indicate how and where the cost might be met. As to where, there is a limited choice: the individual property owners, the occupants of the detailed Study Area whether their property is affected or not, the people of the city as a whole (district ratepayers), the people of the Administrative area (county ratepayers) or the general public of the nation (taxpayers). As to how, this could be expressed in terms of a lump sum grant; or as the same figure spread over the anticipated period of implementation, 15 years; or it could be money raised by an initial loan, repayable over a period of years in the manner of a mortgage by interest and capital combined. Some local authorities take loans for a period of 60 to 80 years but it was thought to be more realistic and in line with current financial practice to show a loan repayment period of 15 years, since, as indicated above, there is some reason to suppose that an acceptable conservation programme might be implemented by private enterprise.

Who pays?

8.50   It would be possible to implement a scheme of finance which operated on a combination of all three — an initial lump sum, partly provided by grant and partly by loan plus a regular lump sum each year for the continuation of the programme. There is, however, an important factor to be considered when devising a scheme of finance and that is the nature of the proposals themselves. These could be sub-divided under numerous headings of 'essential', 'desirable', 'ideal if we can afford it', 'could be omitted' and so on. This is considered irrelevant in the context of a study. What is vital is the difference between proposals which form the framework of the programme and those which merely clothe that frame with better quality bricks and mortar. The latter proposals are meaningless without the former and it is because of this that the costs of the communal works and the individual works have been shown separately. The communal works are the base or frame and must be implemented early and in their entirety. It would be impracticable to attempt the phasing out of expenditure under this heading and the effect is shown in the first part of Table V. The second part of the table gives some indication of the level of local taxation which would be required to provide finance for the various schemes. The effect on national resources would be negligible and is not shown, while it is assumed that private enterprise implementation would look towards loan in the first instance followed by the provision, from public funds, of sufficient to cover the deficit and costs.

Table V
Who pays?

	DEFICIT	Spread over 15 years	Loan repayments over 15 years
From Table II (see Note 2)	£101,460	—	£11,494 p.a.
	£185,250	£12,350 p.a. or	£20,986 p.a.
	£286,710		**£32,480** p.a.
From Tables III & IV	**£59,560**	£3,970 p.a. or	**£6,747** p.a.

		County	City	Study Area
Rate required to produce	£32,480 p.a.	0.3d.	7.3d.	10/9.4d.
Rate required to produce	£6,747 p.a.	0.06d.	1.5d.	2/2.9d.

Note 1   Each annual repayment of loan includes Principal and Interest, the latter being taken at the rate of $7\frac{1}{2}$%.

Summary

8.51   The Study, where it deals with existing buildings, indicates little or no obviously valuable piece of property exploitation that could be carried out and rarely does the existing use of the occupied site fall short of its value for clearance and development. On the other hand, the proposals for the more profitable use of bare land, which may have originated on aesthetic grounds such as completing an unsatisfactory street scene, have made an appreciable difference to the economic outcome.

8.52   For the reasons given, no attempt has been made to quantify any difference in value that may occur on account of the altered environment in the area. It is possible that some added capital appreciation will arise in most of the property within the detailed Study Area, whether physically affected or not; it is equally possible that some measure of depreciation may occur outside the Study Area but whether this might be within the city or a much wider area is a matter for conjecture.

8.53   It is seldom that the conversion of unused commercial accommodation to residential use can be justified on economic grounds alone.

8.54   Current legislation is not conducive to making the maximum use of property and the actions of various Governments in arbitrarily imposing statutory requirements on the normal processes of bargaining between landlord and tenant more frequently hinder than help. If an occupier does brave all the problems and improves his property he will have the dubious pleasure of paying for it annually in the form of additional rates.

8.55   Fragmentation of ownership is the major impediment to the best use of property and to the implementation of works affecting several properties simultaneously.

8.56   Conventional methods of collecting betterment are wasteful of capital and cumbersome. Central and local government authorities are reluctant to spend large amounts of public funds in the acquisition of properties solely in order to put betterment into the public purse. In the alternative they are equally reluctant to provide grants which permit individual property owners to benefit at the expense of the general public.

Statistics

(1) Present capital value of all freehold interests	£3,615,020
(2) Present capital value of all known leasehold interests	205,550
(3) Enhancement in value (betterment) due to communal works	10,450
(4) Enhancement in value (betterment) due to individual works	82,100
(5) Capital value of land after release of Development Value	172,250
(6) Injury to value due to communal works	26,700
(7) Injury to value due to individual works	46,750
(8) Construction cost of communal works	63,095
(9) Construction cost of individual works	162,415
(10) Betterment which can be set-off against injury	5,700
(11) Injury which can be set-off against betterment	2,200
(12) Capital value of interests where betterment exceeds injury (31 properties)	604,400
(13) Trade disturbance to properties included in (12) above	83,800
(14) Existing use value of land considered by (5) above	28,900
(15) Estimated Rental Value of all property in the Study Area	per annum 278,404
(16) Gross Value for rating of all hereditaments in the Study Area	77,944
(17) Rateable Value of all hereditaments in the Study Area	60,344
(18) Estimated cost of buildings which could be erected on 'development land'	375,000

	numbers of
(19) Freehold interests valued at least once	145
(20) Leasehold interests valued at least once	36
(21) Properties affected by (a) communal works only	28
(22) (b) individual works only	35
(23) (c) both	53
(24) Rateable hereditaments:	206
(25) Crown exemptions:	2
(26) Product of 1d. rate in Administrative County of West Sussex	103,905
(27) Product of 1d. rate in Chichester City	4,470
(28) Product of 1d. rate in detailed Study Area	251

9 Method and Procedure

Method and procedure in Chichester

9.01 Of the four special studies of historic towns those of Bath, Chester, and York were prepared by private consultants, but that of Chichester was undertaken by the County Planning Officer who acted as consultant. This was found to have many advantages. The background information was readily available. Members of the County Planning Department staff who were engaged on the study already possessed considerable local knowledge. They were familiar with recent changes and current tendencies in the locality, and were in close contact with individuals or local organisations who were well informed in respect of certain features of the city and/or aspects of its life and character. It was possible to guide certain development proposed during the period of the Study, and subsequently, on the lines which were considered to be desirable as a result of the Study. As County Hall is in Chichester, field work could be readily carried out, and facts easily established or checked at all stages of the Study. For varying periods of time it was possible to draw on a wide range of staff from other departments in County Hall (such as those of the County Architect, County Surveyor and County Valuer), who had differing skills and abilities, and also possessed considerable local knowledge.

Composition of the team

9.02 The team generally consisted of five members at any one time, including the leader, two qualified members, one of intermediate standard and one junior, although these were, with the exception of the leader and the partially qualified member, changed as differing abilities were required. Other members of County Hall staff were employed for varying lengths of time. One completely new member of the staff was appointed to the team, and this may have offset the possible disadvantage resulting from other members of the team having too great a familiarity with the city and its planning problems. Students, members of youth clubs and school children also gave assistance in large scale surveys.

Time taken for the study

9.03 The length of time taken for the Study in Chichester was influenced by many varying factors. Nine months were allocated for the completion of the report, including the preparation of illustrations in a form suitable for reproduction by Her Majesty's Stationery Office. Work had already begun on a detailed study along the lines proposed in *Chichester – Preservation and Progress* and the Town Centre Map, which were submitted as supporting documents to the Reviewed Development Plan, (4.02), and which formed the basis for the Study.

P

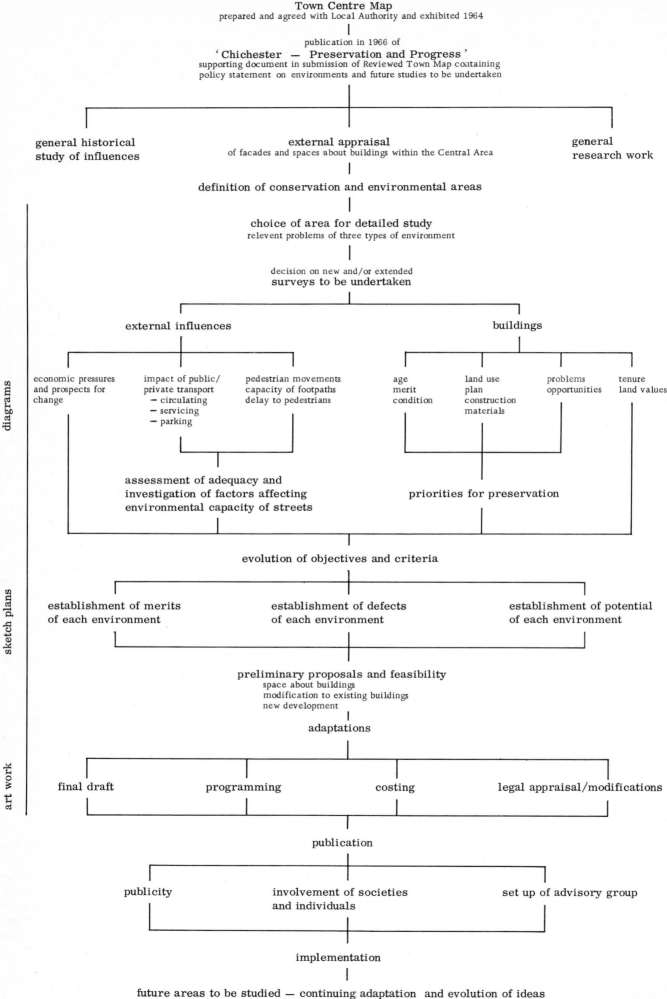

Town Centre Map
prepared and agreed with Local Authority and exhibited 1964

publication in 1966 of
'Chichester — Preservation and Progress'
supporting document in submission of Reviewed Town Map containing
policy statement on environments and future studies to be undertaken

general historical
study of influences

external appraisal
of facades and spaces about buildings within the Central Area

general
research work

definition of conservation and environmental areas

choice of area for detailed study
relevent problems of three types of environment

decision on new and/or extended
surveys to be undertaken

external influences

buildings

economic pressures
and prospects for
change

impact of public/
private transport
— circulating
— servicing
— parking

pedestrian movements
capacity of footpaths
delay to pedestrians

age
merit
condition

land use
plan
construction
materials

problems
opportunities

tenure
land values

diagrams

assessment of adequacy and
investigation of factors affecting
environmental capacity of streets

priorities for preservation

evolution of objectives and criteria

establishment of merits
of each environment

establishment of defects
of each environment

establishment of potential
of each environment

sketch plans

preliminary proposals and feasibility
space about buildings
modification to existing buildings
new development

adaptations

final draft

programming

costing

legal appraisal/modifications

art work

publication

publicity

involvement of societies
and individuals

set up of advisory group

implementation

future areas to be studied — continuing adaptation and evolution of ideas

continuing meetings with City representatives and interdepartmental discussions

In the early part of the period allocated for the Study, about a month was devoted to the Inquiry into the Reviewed Development Plan proposals. The time taken for the actual survey of individual properties (6.21) varied a great deal, especially as some properties had to be visited more than once, to suit the convenience of the occupiers. It was felt that it was best for two people to visit each property, since this resulted not only in greater speed, but also in a more balanced assessment of qualitative factors. It was found that an average of three medium-size properties could be visited each day.

9.04   A study of another similar area of Chichester would, it is estimated, take only three or four months with a team of similar size, since a great deal of background material relevant to the whole town has been obtained, and effective methods and procedure have been established (7.159).

Method of study

9.05   The accompanying diagram (fig. 123) illustrates the method by which the Study was carried out, following the preparation of the Reviewed Development Plan, with the Town Centre Map and the publication *Chichester — Preservation and Progress* (4.02).

Ways and means of achieving objectives

9.06   If a conservation scheme is to succeed, it is essential that there should be a wide degree of favourable public understanding, and willing co-operation on the parts of owners and occupiers directly affected. An exhibition is probably the most effective means of putting the recommendations clearly and comprehensively before the public. Large scale maps and diagrams, with coloured perspectives or elevations, are easier to understand than the much smaller scale illustrative material, with its limited range of colours, which can be included in this report. Furthermore, an exhibition staffed by members of the local authority planning department would provide an excellent opportunity for individual questions to be asked and answered, and points to be made directly to members of the public with the aid of the displayed material.

9.07   Because of the number of properties (approximately 160) in the Study Area, it is not practicable to include in the report detailed recommendations affecting each property. These could be made available on request by interested parties at an exhibition, and could always be made known on enquiry at the local planning authority offices. It is always desirable to stress the long-term benefits to the area as a whole which would result from the course of action recommended, since the effects of this would fall unevenly on individual owners and occupiers.

9.08   Consideration will be given to the setting up of an Advisory Group or panel of experts whose duty would be to help residents of the Conservation Area on varying problems relating to their property, and to guide changes or development within the area along the lines laid down in this report. The law and regulations relating to planning are extremely complicated, especially concerning the ways and means of obtaining financial assistance for the preservation or renovation of buildings. An excellent booklet on the subject has been published by Cambridgeshire and Isle of Ely County Council*. It is suggested that a

*A Guide to Historic Buildings Law, published by Cambridgeshire and Isle of Ely County Council, County Planning Department, 1967

further pamphlet be produced indicating in broad outline the best courses of procedure and the liabilities placed on owners of listed properties, in a manner easily understandable by the general public. General advice might also be available from the suggested Advisory Group on problems relating to alterations, repair and maintenance of old properties, external colour schemes, lettering on buildings, lighting effects, the treatment of surfaces around buildings and urban landscaping. Excellent work has already been done on individual properties, and names of persons who specialise in these fields would be made available. A concise guide booklet including information on notable buildings and other features of historic interest could be commissioned by the Group. They might also give encouragement and advice on the planting of trees, especially where existing trees are likely to be felled due to age or proposed development. Another duty of the Advisory Group might be to ensure that, when old buildings are demolished, materials suitable for re-use and architectural features of note are carefully preserved for use in repairing and renovating other buildings (7.124).

9.09   The actual composition of such a group or panel, the scope of its duties, the location of its accommodation, the means of payments to its members and other factors would have to be discussed and agreed by various societies and individuals who would be interested in the project. It would be appropriate for the local authorities concerned to give a lead, but it is thought that the Civic Society and other allied organisations should sponsor the scheme, use their influence to make the public aware of conservation problems and act as general 'watch-dogs'. The citizens of Chichester would be encouraged to take a civic pride in their heritage in order to ensure that the best total environment is achieved for the benefit of the community as a whole, in an atmosphere of good neighbourliness and co-operation. With initiative and foresight, much can be achieved by local authorities, societies, and individuals within the city, with the minimum of expenditure.

Suggested method where a Town Centre Map has not been prepared

9.10   In Chichester, the preparation of a Town Centre Map preceded the definition of a Conservation Area (5.01). In another town where a Conservation Area within the central area is contemplated, but for which no Town Centre Map has been prepared, it would be appropriate for the studies leading to the definition of a Conservation Area (or Conservation Areas) to be carried out in conjunction with the survey for the Town Centre Map.

9.11   The procedure suggested for the formulation of proposals and policies for Conservation Areas in conjunction with Town Centre Maps is as follows:
(a) Contact with local civic, amenity or preservation societies
(b) Preliminary appraisal of the environment
(c) Delineation of draft Conservation Areas
(d) Completion of draft Town Centre Map, indicating draft Conservation Areas
(e) Detailed study of Conservation Areas
(f) Completion of definitive Town Centre Map, together with statement of conservation policy and specific proposals for part or all of the proposed Conservation Areas.

Contact with local societies

9.12   If there are local civic, amenity or preservation societies, it is desirable to make contact with these at the outset of a conservation study. Such bodies often includes members with considerable local knowledge in architectural or historical matters and may be of great help in providing background information. They may also be of assistance in various other ways during the course of the study, including possibly direct participation in the survey by individual members. They could provide a valuable link between the planning authority and people living and working in the area. Collaboration between planning authorities and local societies can also result in the better mutual understanding of planning aims and procedure, and of the problems and conflicts which arise in the course of the control of development in historic towns.

Preliminary appraisal of the environment

9.13   A visual assessment of the town centre would be undertaken by means of a field survey. The townscape of every street and significant space would be recorded by means of quick annotated sketches (fig. 34) and note would be taken of areas with special architectural or historical quality.

9.14   A preliminary environmental analysis would then be carried out. Distinct environmental areas would be identified and delineated on a map. Not all the environmental areas so identified would necessarily have a strong, positive character; some might have no particular visual distinction but might be identifiable because of a dominant type of activity, or because of their topography. Other areas might have little or no distinctive quality. The boundaries of environmental areas might sometimes have to be drawn arbitrarily, even through groups of buildings (such as shop premises facing a busy street, but backing onto a servicing area with a completely different environmental character).

Delineation of draft Conservation Areas

9.15   Conservation areas should then be broadly defined, to include environmental areas which have good, or potentially good, visual character or special historical interest. Intermediate or adjoining areas of less positive quality might also be included, if it appeared that these were capable of improvement, in conjunction with the areas of more distinct character.

Completion of draft Town Centre Map

9.16   The preliminary appraisal of the environment, leading to the delineation of the draft Conservation Areas, would be undertaken in conjunction with the general survey for the first draft of the Town Centre Map. The outline planning proposals for the Town Centre would take account of the draft Conservation Areas, and these would be indicated on the draft Town Centre Map.

9.17   At this stage it might be thought appropriate to hold an exhibition, and/or to publish a simple, well illustrated booklet explaining the aims of the conservation study as well as the outline proposals for the Town Centre. It is recognised that there are certain dangers in publicising draft proposals which have not yet been made precise, since this may lead to uncertainty as to the effect of planning proposals on existing properties. However, this disadvantage would be more than compensated by increased interest and understanding of conservation problems by members of the public.

Detailed study of Conservation Areas

9.18   After the completion of the draft Town Centre Map, further survey work would begin, leading to the preparation of a final Town Centre Map.

9.19   At the same time, an environmental re-assessment of the draft Conservation Areas should be undertaken. Each street or section of the Conservation Areas should be examined systematically, in order to evaluate the environmental qualities of each (whether good, indifferent or bad), to highlight the conservation problems, and to assess, as far as possible, the nature of the work (including further survey work) which it would be necessary to undertake in the pursuance of an effective conservation policy. It is recommended that this re-assessment be carried out on the lines suggested in Chapter 5 (5.27), using the type of form illustrated in figure 47.

9.20   A broad conservation programme should then be determined, in conjunction with the formulation of detailed policies for the draft Town Centre Map. A decision should be reached as to which properties in each Conservation Area it would be desirable to investigate in detail, and how much of this survey work it would be appropriate to carry out at this stage, having regard to the time and the resources available. In some Conservation Areas it might be considered necessary to survey every property in detail before deciding on a conservation policy; in others it might be more appropriate to investigate only a proportion of the properties. The aim should be to obtain significant tangible results in a fairly short time, possibly within a restricted area, rather than spread effort and resources too thinly over a wide field.

9.21   A detailed study of properties should then be undertaken according to the priorities determined in the conservation programme (9.28). It is suggested that a form similar to that in figures 59 and 60 (6.22) be used, accompanied by sketch plans of the buildings investigated.

9.22   At all stages of the conservation study financial considerations should be fully examined.

Town Centre Map with conservation policy and proposals

9.23   The completed Town Centre Map would indicate the defined Conservation Areas, and would be accompanied by statements relating to conservation policy, proposals relating to the Conservation Areas, including their programming (in as much detail as possible) and a financial appraisal.

9.24   The maximum publicity should be given to the proposals, through exhibitions, publications and other appropriate means. A real understanding of the objectives and methods of conservation by the general public (particularly those who would be directly affected), and by local civic, amenity and preservation societies is necessary if a conservation programme is to be successfully carried through.

Conservation procedure and principles applicable to towns and villages generally

9.25   Every Conservation Area will have its own particular characteristics, problems and needs, calling for specific courses of action. However, it is possible to set out broadly the nature of the material which needs to be studied, assessed and analysed, and the factors which should generally guide the formulation of policies and principles in respect of Conservation Areas generally, and this is done in the subsequent paragraphs. Much of this material is repetitive, in summarised form, of the survey, analysis and recommendations in respect of Chichester, but note is also taken of factors which are less specifically applicable to Chichester. It is hoped that this section will be useful for reference in connection with conservation studies in other areas *.

Preliminary considerations

9.26   The significance of a Conservation Area in a town or village should be firmly established, against the background of planned or expected development within both the place itself and its dependent hinterland. In an expanding community, a Conservation Area might be deliberately preserved as an area with relatively little physical change, though possibly changing in its functions. In a relatively static town or village the functions might remain little altered, but physical improvements might be desirable. Elsewhere, both physical improvements and functional charges might be considered necessary. The appropriate course would depend upon the circumstances of each case; existing economic and social pressures and tendencies should be assessed and decisions reached as to whether such trends should be encouraged, resisted or diverted, or new trends engendered. Too much economic pressure on an area might lead to too great a tendency towards rapid change; conversely, too little pressure might lead to under-use or disuse of buildings, with consequent decay (1.06).

9.27   An important factor which should be taken into account in the planning of an historic town is tourism, the present and potential significance of which should be assessed where practicable. The attraction to tourists of a well conserved historic area could be an added incentive for expenditure on conservation.

Uses and activities

9.28   When it has been decided which properties within a Conservation Area should be investigated, a detailed survey of each property should be undertaken, in order to ascertain its uses and activities, as well as its structural and architectural characteristics. For this purpose it is not sufficient to define uses within the normal broad categories, such as residential, industrial, shopping, public open spaces, civic or business. The precise nature of each use, in each property, must be assessed, and it is often necessary to analyse the disposition of particular uses within particular properties. For instance, it may be very relevant to find which parts of a shop premises are used for selling, which parts for storage, which parts for other ancillary purposes such as facilities for staff, and whether any parts of the building or associated space are disused or under-used, as well as the number of people employed and the means of access for customers, staff and goods. Similarly, in the case of residential properties, it is usually desirable to find the extent of occupation by individual households (if the property is subdivided), and the extent (if any) of

*See appendix B at the end of the report for Analysis and Check List of data for Conservation Areas.

disuse or under-use of the buildings and associated spaces, as well as the composition of each household and the means of access to each residential unit.

9.29 The overall pattern of uses in each environmental area should be assessed, and a decision reached as to whether the present pattern is generally appropriate, having regard to the character of the environment. It may be thought desirable to plan for a change in the general pattern of uses, with certain existing uses being retained and developed, new uses introduced, and other existing uses discouraged or eliminated.

9.30 Once the desirable future general pattern of uses in a particular area has been determined, the suitability of existing uses in each individual property should be assessed, and consideration given to desirable uses for properties which are unsuitably used or vacant. Assessment should then be made as to whether alterations or adaptations are required in such existing property for its present or future use and, if it is a building of notable architectural or historical quality, how such alterations could be carried out without detracting from, put possibly enhancing, its character. Finding suitable uses for old buildings worthy of preservation sometimes presents difficult problems, but solutions can usually be found if imagination is used, and the buildings are considered in relation to their existing or potential environment (7.140).

9.31 Uses and activities associated with new development (9.47) should be considered in relation to those existing, and to the future environmental pattern.

9.32 The dominant future use or uses for each section of a Conservation Area would thus be determined, but this should not necessarily imply rigid 'zoning'. In the control of development in Conservation Areas, firmness is necessary in order to exclude uses and activities which are environmentally undesirable, but flexibility is also needed so that appropriate uses (which may not correspond to the intended dominant uses, but which are not detrimental to the environment as a whole) can be found for individual properties.

Vehicular and pedestrian movements

9.33 A Conservation Area plan should make provision, as far as is practicable or desirable, for the segregation of pedestrian and vehicular traffic, and for the separation of differing degrees of traffic (through traffic, visiting traffic and service traffic), avoiding detriment to areas of high environmental quality. Heavy traffic flows through main shopping streets or other streets of special significance or character are now unacceptable. Widening of such streets, or the introduction of one-way traffic, tend to increase the speed and flow of traffic and hence the danger to pedestrians and detriment to the environment. The environmental capacity of each street should be assessed (6.95) and the future traffic pattern designed so that this capacity is nowhere exceeded.

9.34 The desirability of creating pedestrian precincts in many types of environment, particularly in shopping centres, has been sufficiently well established and widely accepted, particularly since the publication of Professor Buchanan's *Traffic in Towns* (3.88), so that no further general justification is necessary. However, pedestrian precincts are not necessarily always appropriate in the shopping centres of towns; sometimes a small amount of traffic can be visually stimulating and not detrimental to the environment. It has sometimes been stated that the creation of pedestrian precincts, or the substantial reduction of traffic in a shopping centre, results in loss of trade. This has not however always proved to be the case.

9.35 If a pedestrian precinct is to be formed in an existing shopping centre, it is necessary to provide adequate servicing provision for all the properties affected. Usually this requires the creation of new service roads and servicing areas. In some cases this could not be achieved without serious detriment to the environmental quality of an adjoining area, or without the costly demolition of substantial buildings. Compromise would then be necessary, possibly by allowing the existing shopping street to remain open for servicing vehicles only, maybe at restricted times. In streets where the retention of some traffic is unavoidable, pedestrian priority might be established as a matter of general principle, with crossings at frequent intervals, indicated perhaps by means other than the statutory flashing signs. Patterns for future shopping and servicing provision should be reasonably flexible, since it is difficult to ascertain future trends with precision. Changes in shopping habits (such as more shopping being done by post) and in patterns of servicing (resulting from the possible development of a centralised warehousing system) would affect the amount of provision needed in particular towns.

9.36 Garaging must be provided for residential properties. It is worth noting however, that residential uses normally generate less traffic than commercial or other uses in comparable properties, and this is a factor which should be taken into account when assessing the amount of future residential occupation within a Conservation Area. Parking provision for commuters need not always be in close proximity to the place of employment. The future pattern of general parking should be planned in relation to the town centre as a whole, and would not necessarily include provision within a Conservation Area.

9.37 It is important to decide the future pattern of public transport when planning a Conservation Area. Large buses can be intrusive in many environments, but convenient public transport must be provided if people are not to be unduly encouraged to bring private cars into a busy centre. Methods of public transport which are in scale and keeping with the environment, connecting with longer distance public transport (and possibly with car parks), should be considered for town centres of special historical character. In any event it is desirable to improve the 'image' of public transport, and to encourage its use as much as possible. If subsidies are necessary in order to provide an adequate service, their cost must be weighed against the environmental deterioration which results from increased volumes of private cars.

Spaces and buildings

9.38 Factors which contribute to good or bad townscape should be studied and analysed in detail. They are, however, very numerous and complex, and can only be summarised briefly in the present context.

Ground surfaces

9.39 The form and pattern of the ground surfaces of spaces should be studied in relation to the functions of the spaces and the movements through them. Note should be taken of the varying colour and textural quality of surfaces including, for example, the varying visual effects of unbroken stretches of a single surfacing material, or those obtained from the patterning of surfaces which are composed of small units. Effects of changing levels, the relationship of the layout and surfacing of spaces to the topography, and the visual significance of grass, flowers and small-scale vegetation should all be assessed. Note should also be taken of the visually disruptive effect of yellow or white painting on road surfaces (which may be required under existing law if parking is to be eliminated or controlled in particular streets).

9.40   Changes in the form, texture and pattern of surfacing materials, and of the system of levels, can often alter the apparent scale of spaces, and hence of the buildings which define or enclose them. This is a consideration which is likely to arise particularly when an existing traffic street is converted into a pedestrian precinct, and the asphalt of carriageways and pavements is substituted by surface materials of different character.

Street furniture
9.41   The visual effect, and practical necessity, of all features such as traffic signs, lighting fixtures, shelters, seats, kiosks, walls, fences, and overhead wires should be studied. If they are intrusive in their present form, but necessary, consideration should be given to re-designing and/or resiting them. Sometimes the introduction of features within spaces, suitably designed and sited, is desirable for visual reasons, in order to give more appropriate scale to the spaces. The value of walls, both in helping to provide definition to spaces, and as features with attractive scale and texture in their own right, must also be considered.

Trees
9.42   Every tree in a Conservation Area should be noted, and its townscape value assessed. A conservation scheme should, if appropriate, include comprehensive proposals for tree planting both in places where it is desirable to introduce trees (either as positive townscape features or, more negatively, in order to conceal or soften the impact of unattractive features which have to be retained), and as replacements for old trees as they near the end of their lives. Where there are large numbers of trees, tree planting and replacement should be a continuous process, and it is recommended that the establishment of 'tree banks' should be considered, so that trees of suitable species, age and size are available when needed. In any case the advice of an arboriculturalist should be sought on the planting, maintenance, replacement or removal of trees.

9.43   Trees are not always appropriate in townscapes, especially in close built, intensely urban streets. Their value as foils to buildings must, however, always be considered. Sometimes a single tree conspicuous in a street acts as an excellent foil, or a group of trees effectively sets off an adjoining group of buildings.

9.44   In most urban environments, trees should be of the traditional, large scale species. There are many varieties of small trees which are appropriate in suburban environments, but not in town centres.

The collective visual character of buildings
9.45   There are so many factors to be taken into account relating to the collective visual character of buildings, that they have been summarised in note form.
(a) The scale, shape and proportions of buildings. Height, uniform or varied; if varied, the range of variations. Skyline, regular or varied; form of roofs; prevalence of cornices, eaves, parapets, gables or other endings to elevations. Proportions of facades, and of window and door openings, shop fronts and other features in relation to the whole; vertical and/or horizontal emphasis. Significance of

buildings or architectural features which are markedly different in scale, shape or proportions to the others, providing contrasts; whether such contrasts are acceptable (e.g. where small buildings act as effective foils to larger buildings, or tall or prominent buildings provide 'punctuation'), or visually disturbing.

(b) The architectural character of buildings. Uniformity, prevalence of one style with some variation, or mixture of styles. The effect of variations, attractive or disruptive. Types of windows (e.g. mullioned, sash, casement, plate glass); doorways and other significant features. Importance of detailing (e.g. mouldings, stringcourses, hoods, canopies, balconies, pediments, barge-boards) in the group effect. Assessment of local architectural traditions (which may have varied over different periods). Assessment of value of groups of buildings in exemplifying architectural characteristics which are typical of a period or a locality, in providing unique, unusual or specially remarkable examples of certain types of development.

(c) Building materials, colour and texture. The range of materials; uniform or varied; degree of variety. Appreciation of the range of building materials traditional in the locality (the prevalence of each may have varied over different periods). Colour and textural effects; those which are inherent in the materials used and those which are applied; harmonious or disruptive effects.

(d) The disposition of buildings. Frontages continuous or broken; effects of breaks in the continuity of groups of buildings (positive or disruptive). Frontages straight or otherwise; effects of changes in alignment (recessions, projections, curves whether regular or haphazard); special significance of particular buildings because of their position in the townscape. Changing effects from different viewpoints (buildings appear in different visual relationship with each other, and with adjoining spaces, when seen from different angles, and individual buildings may have varying townscape importance depending upon the viewpoint). Interest created by corners, curving streets and entry into new environments. Effects of enclosure of spaces provided by buildings; closure and 'punctuation' of significant vistas and where this is lacking and needed. Effects of vistas or of glimpses of other spaces, buildings or features, seen through gaps between buildings. Inter-relationship of buildings and spaces; effect and apparent scale of buildings enhanced or reduced by expanse, scale, shape or design of spaces adjoining them; effect and scale of spaces influenced by the siting, scale and appearance of buildings defining them.

Survey of individual buildings

9.46 In the survey of individual buildings it is necessary to note the following features (also summarised because of the number of the factors involved).

(a) The form of each building. Number of storeys (including basements and attics); disposition of rooms on each storey; means of access and of internal circulation; heights of rooms (especially where these are abnormally great or small); position of chimney-breasts and chimneys; form of roofs; form and disposition of windows, and their adequacy.

(b) The construction of each building. Materials used in various parts (these may not always be obvious or visible); thickness of walls and of other features where this seems significant; the degree to which walls and other features are load-bearing; form of the structural framework (where buildings are timber-framed); nature and adequacy of foundations (where this is possible to ascertain). Relevant factors which are particular to a locality, such as the nature of the subsoil and local traditions in the construction of buildings, should be studied. Note should also be taken of evidence of additions and alterations to buildings at various times, and the effects these may have had on the earlier structures.

(c) The condition of each building. Evidence of disrepair, serious or superficial; evidence of structural faults, particularly in walls or other constructional features which are load bearing; the causes of structural faults (decay in materials, attack by fungus or insects, overloading, alterations to load bearing features, demolition of adjoining structures, new materials in conjunction with old, excessive heat or dampness, vibration from traffic or other causes, atmospheric pollution). The urgency of the need for repairs or structural alterations should be assessed.

(d) The intrinsic architectural or historical value of each building (as distinct from its townscape value). The age of each part; the extent to which the building, or each distinct part of the building, is a significant or valuable example of its type and period, in the national, regional or local context; the extent to which the architectural or historical value of the building, or part of the building, may have been reduced or enhanced by alterations; the visual effect of the materials, in terms of colour and texture; the significance of detailed features on the exterior; the importance of period features inside. Note should be made of possible ways in which the character of the building might be enhanced through alterations, redecoration, or the reinstatement of old features which have been removed. Note should also be taken of individual features which might be re-used elsewhere or stored for future use if for any reason retention in their present position were impracticable.

New buildings

9.47 Although, in a Conservation Area, the emphasis will be on preserving groups of buildings of architectural interest, there are likely to be many instances where the erection of new buildings would be required, or would be desirable in order to improve the environment. Generally they should be in the idiom of the day, but harmonious with the existing environment in scale, proportions and texture. Often it is possible and desirable to use traditional materials; if new materials are to be used, their visual effect in relation to the older buildings should be taken into account. Sometimes, however, especially where there is an existing uniformity of design (as in a planned Georgian street or square) it might be legitimate to build in imitation of the existing design.

9.48 The erection of new structures in Conservation Areas may sometimes be desirable for visual reasons as, for instance, to fill an intrusive gap in a group of buildings or to give firmer definition to a space; in other instances new development may be appropriate in order to introduce new uses and activities within an area (such as residential uses in areas which have become largely commercial), which would improve the quality of the environment.

Economic considerations

9.49 The economic implications of conservation should be thoroughly assessed and these should influence the formulation of policy and proposals within the Conservation Area. The 'balance sheet' of every course of action which is considered should be drawn out, offsetting existing values of properties, and their potential under present circumstances, against their value after the conservation proposals have been taken into account. Sometimes conservation policy will result in an effective loss of potential value, and many courses of action proposed in Conservation Areas are not likely to be directly profitable in themselves (such as improvements to the exterior of buildings, improvements to the appearance of spaces, and costly preservation of individual buildings because of their architectural value). However, in many cases, as when existing under-used or unsuitably used buildings and spaces are put to more beneficial use, there may be a direct gain in property value. Furthermore, conservation should lead to long term gains resulting from the improvement in the environment, which would eventually be reflected in increase in property values. Such improvement would effect the prosperity of the entire town, which would become more attractive for residence, or for regular or occasional visitors.

9.50 Conservation studies and programmes are initiated by local authorities, so that expenditure on them must be largely financed from local resources. Some grants are available (7.139). In the long run and under the present system, such expenditure would be partly compensated by an overall increase in rateable value as a result of additional amenities, but revised legislation is necessary if effective conservation policies are to be carried out (8.38). The shortage of craftsmen with the necessary skills for the improvement or maintenance of old buildings, the rising cost of their employment and the high cost of certain traditional materials, are likely to present problems for many local authorities. This might be partly overcome by organising a 'pool' of craftsmen, and a co-ordinated supply of materials, in connection with conservation work over a wide area. Shortage of professional staff may also present difficulties, but this could be partly offset by securing the interest and help of civic and amenity societies (9.12).

Conclusion

9.51 Attractive historical environments should be conserved because they are irreplaceable (they could not be reproduced satisfactorily in modern times under contemporary conditions), because they are records of historical change, and because they offer such rich contrasts with modern environments (1.04). At the same time, they must be adapted to present day needs and requirements, and made relevant to the activities of the locality in which they are set, without losing their essential historic and visually attractive character. No urban environment is ever static, and it is desirable, in the process of conservation, to encourage those pressures and trends which contribute towards the improvement of historical environments, and to counteract those which tend in the opposite direction (1.06). Emphasis should be on the positive aspects of conservation rather than on the more negative effects of pure preservation of individual buildings.

10 Summary of findings

Summary of Findings

10.01 **A conservation policy** must be formulated against the background of a comprehensive plan.

10.02 **Some conservation on a limited scale** has been achieved through private or public enterprise and investment. This indicates what could be achieved with a comprehensive policy.

10.03 **Factors adversely affecting environment include:**
(a) Impact of traffic
(b) Inappropriate use (or under-use) of buildings and land
(c) Buildings which are inappropriate for their settings because of scale, proportions, details, or external treatment
(d) Deficiencies in the relationship between buildings and spaces (e.g. breaks in an otherwise continuous frontage)
(e) Badly designed or sited street furniture and intrusive advertising
(f) Unsatisfactory treatment of ground surfaces.

10.04 **Separation of pedestrian and vehicular routes** is desirable, particularly in shopping centres. Successive surveys have confirmed this.

10.05 **Guided change and preservation** are the essential components of conservation. To preserve old buildings satisfactorily, it is often necessary to adapt them to new requirements. New buildings, and new activities are often needed in conservation areas, and must be integrated into the old environment.

10.06 **Office development in a residential environment** (preferably of the professional rather than the commercial type) can sometimes be accepted, provided the residential character of the area is preserved.

10.07 **New residential use** helps to improve the character of an historic central area, especially in vacant upper floors. Low traffic generation is an added advantage.

10.08 **The character of buildings,** including their uses, construction and architectural value and condition can be fully appreciated only after detailed investigation. Consideration of the use of buildings should be inseparable from study of the other factors.

10.09 **Under-use of property** (particularly upper floors) is a major factor contributing to decay. In many commercial premises, upper floors are unlikely to be used unless there is some financial inducement.

10.10 **Special knowledge and skills** are needed for the adaptation and conversion of old buildings. Needless damage is caused through failure to appreciate the construction of old buildings. Serious cases of disrepair in buildings call for urgent action.

10.11   **Old materials suitable for re-use** in repairs, reinstatement or alterations should be preserved and stored.

10.12   **An extended system of listing** buildings of architectural and historical interest is desirable, to include a wider range, and to take greater account of environmental considerations.

10.13   **New buildings must be sympathetic** in proportions, detailing and materials, and should generally be in the idiom of the day. Designing in past styles is sometimes justifiable in townscapes of uniform character, or for small scale alterations to buildings.

10.14   **Car parking space** can often be satisfactorily provided within a conservation area, if special attention is given to the visual treatment of the space and to access arrangements.

10.15   **New legislation relating to traffic signs** and markings is needed if their intrusive effect on the environment is to be minimised. A composite sign at each entrance to a conservation area would be desirable.

10.16   **Existing legislation is inappropriate** for the implementation of conservation proposals, which could be achieved today only by an extensive programme of compulsory acquisition dispossessing the occupiers. Not only would this be unacceptable, but the administration and financial burdens placed upon the implementing authority would be excessive.

10.17   **In the absence of statutory powers** to secure the repair of property, financial inducements must be made, in the form of grants or loans to owners and occupiers from national or local bodies.

10.18   **Recovery of betterment** (obtained from increased property values through development or improvement) is impracticable under present legislation. If enhanced values through conservation could be recovered for re-investment in other conservation work, the net costs of a conservation programme would be much reduced.

10.19   **New legislation is needed** to enable the implementing authority either to purchase without dispossessing the occupiers, or to carry out compulsorily necessary works of improvement (compensating for losses where they occur, and recovering betterment). Fragmentation of ownership is a major impediment to the implementation of a comprehensive conservation scheme.

10.20   **Conservation trusts** are suggested, which would enable owners and occupiers to be more closely involved in the process of conservation.

10.21   **A phased conservation programme** for restoration, adaptation, improvement or renewal should be made, having regard to resources available.

10.22   **Swift action is necessary** if the character of historic areas is not to be irretrievably lost.

Appendix A

Supplementary rating system for conservation area (8.48)

A system might be devised as a means of providing finance for the types of works not covered by existing legislation, and for those works which it would not be reasonable to expect individual property owners to finance. It would also serve to encourage appropriate uses and discourage inappropriate uses in a conservation Area.

In detail it would be designed to cover the following works:

1 Alterations required on aesthetic grounds in order to reduce the harmful effect of incongruous buildings, e.g. restoration of windows of Georgian proportions where 'improvements' have resulted in the insertion of plate glass.

2 Extra costs of public works where a standard above that normally acceptable is required, e.g. use of old stone flags in preference to new concrete pavings.

3 Fees to advisors.

4 Extra costs of higher than normal maintenance on public property, e.g. close mown grass, more frequent painting, checks for damp in buildings of special importance.

The basis for assessment on each building might be a unit, of, say, one-eightieth of the rateable value multiplied by three sliding-scale indices. These three indices could be based on the following factors:

(a) *Suitability of use* in the environment of the conservation area. Once the dominant character has been established, the most appropriate uses can be decided upon. Buildings used most appropriately would then carry the lowest index under this heading, whilst those used in ways which were most detrimental to the environment would have the highest. Thus in the case of the Chichester conservation area the scale might be:

house	+1
flat	+2
hotel	+3
hostel	+4
office (professional)	+5
office (commercial)	+6
shop (small)	+12
shop (large)	+20
factory (small)	+30
factory (large)	+40

(b) *Property value.* It is suggested that the second index be based on the price range of the property so that those smaller properties, which in the case of Chichester, contribute considerably to the environment carry the least burden. Thus the scale could be:

up to £5,000	+1
£5,000–£10,000	+2
£10,000–£20,000	+4
£20,000–£50,000	+8
over £50,000	+20

(c) *Age of Building.* The third index could be based on the age of properties. The more recent buildings, least in need of costly maintenance (and often those which contribute least to the environment), would carry the heaviest weighting, whereas the oldest buildings would carry the least.

Thus:

Buildings up to 1700	+1
1700 to 1840	+2
1841 to 1900	+4
after 1900	+10

From these three indices a rate could then be formed,

$$\text{R.V.} \frac{(a+b+c)}{(\ 80\ )}$$

e.g. For a Georgian house worth £12,000 of which the rateable value is £200, the supplementary rate would be:

$$200 \frac{(1+4+2)}{(\ 80\ )} = \text{£17 10 0}$$

but for a small modern shop of rateable value £1,000 (perhaps worth £22,000) it would be:

$$1000 \frac{(12+8+10)}{(\ 80\ )} = \text{£375}$$

These products need to be compared with current general rates at about 10s. 0d. in the £, which would yield £100 in the first case and £500 in the second.

It must be acknowledged that the initial assessments would present the usual difficulties of objections and appeals by the ratepayers; collection costs need not be large if the scheme was integrated into the present system of general rate collection.

Appendix B

Analysis and check list of data for Conservation Areas (9.50)

Under the Civic Amenities Act, 1967, the following are intended as a guide to the designation of Conservation Areas:

Page 193 seeks to analyse the content of Conservation Areas and suggests a method for delineating and selecting areas worthy of designation.

Page 194 provides a broad framework and check list for those taking part in conservation work. The work of co-ordination and design will rest with the County Planning Department, but the co-operation of Local Authorities and other Organisations is encouraged so as to promote local involvement in each Conservation Area. The County Planning Department will need to organise much of the survey work but some of this could be undertaken by voluntary organisations (including schools, colleges etc.) and details of availability (time, number, skills etc.) can be added to the check list.

Analysis of Conservation Areas

Part I

Method to be used for the delineation of a Conservation Area in towns and villages

(a) The basis of a conservation area should comprise a group or groups of buildings of architectural or historic merit together with any significant related spaces.

(b) If parts of the original city, town or village have not been destroyed, the conservation area should include sufficient land to contain these.

(c) Where subsequent conflicting activities or insensitive buildings have destroyed the setting of significant buildings or of the relationships between them the conservation area should extend to allow for the recreation of these as far as practicable. Thus conservation work should cater for demolition and/or construction work as well as the restoration or reinstatement of buildings.

Part II

Components of a Conservation Area

(a) Character—the character of the area should be ascertained and where appropriate sub-divided

into various environmental areas, each with its own individual features together with predominant land uses. It may, for example, be an environment containing mixed shopping uses together with a high proportion of buildings which originally formed the mediæval core; an area of mainly good Georgian residential buildings; a car park within the delineated area; or an area of underdeveloped back land which does not constitute an environment but which is associated with one of these areas.

(b) Uses—the proposed uses to which each environment should be put must be ascertained against the overall plan for the area, the social and economic pressures and whether there is any need for change. Policy plans for each conservation area, which have regard to the character or potential character of each environment, can then be prepared in the context of this land use policy.

(c) Pedestrians and vehicles—the extent to which there is conflict between the pedestrian and the vehicular traffic must also be gauged and existing or potential environmental capacity of each street assessed in order to judge the need for any future new roadworks or pedestrian ways. Car parking, means of access and garaging will require investigation and future requirements should be assessed. The public transport system may also be relevant to the preparation of plans.

(d) Details—the individual details of the area need studying before positive proposals can be made. These could contribute to or have a detrimental effect on the area, though in some cases they may merely be nondescript. The areas around buildings (which will include such things as planting, ground surfacing and street furniture) should be included as well as buildings themselves. Historic associations as well as the aesthetic and financial value and the condition of buildings are also important. Materials, texture and colour are of special significance in an historic environment.

(e) Proposals—the conservation area will include creative proposals (which could include new development, re-allocation of uses, alterations or removal of structures) as well as the preservation or restoration of significant buildings. These, together with the economic viability of a scheme and their effect on adjoining areas will be taken into account before any action is taken.

Check list of data for Conservation Area

	Civic Societies	Historic/Archaeological Societies	Church Councils	Architectural Society	Chamber of Commerce	Occupiers of Property	Recreational Associations	Amenity Societies	Local Authority
Historical background									
Archaeological finds in the Conservation Area	■	■							
History of development of Conservation Area	■	■	■						
Details of properties									
Occupier (terms of occupancy)						■			
Owner						■			
Approx. value						■			
Age, structure and condition	■			■		■			
Uses of rooms, land and access details						■			■
Architectural features of note	■			■		■			
Planting and external features of note						■			
Townscape details									
Topography, significant views, links or breaks in scene (river, green etc.)	■	■		■				■	■
Planting (trees, grass etc.)	■							■	
Pavings and hard surfacing, ponds, walls, fences, street furniture, milestones etc. (include quality and condition).	■	■		■		■		■	
Local demand									
Housing						■			■
Shopping, office, tourism etc.					■	■	■		■
Recreation—playing fields, bridle paths, yacht basins etc.							■	■	■
Community activities—halls, theatre, rooms, etc. including land around (include recent development and applications under consideration as well as requirements).			■		■		■	■	■
Movements									
Historic routes (pilgrim ways etc.)	■	■						■	
Existing pattern of roads, bridle paths, canals, etc.								■	■
Present traffic/servicing/parking/garaging problems					■	■	■	■	■
Traffic solutions under consideration (include pedestrians, horses, bicycles, light and heavy vehicles, buses—regular services and coaches—trains, boats, aircraft).	■					■	■	■	■
Local conservation proposals									
Restorations and improvements recently carried out by private individuals or Civic Trust schemes	■			■					
Suggestions for individual improvements	■		■	■	■		■	■	■
Suggestions for conservation plans	■			■	■			■	■
Details of possible local finance which may be available.	■	■	■	■	■	■	■	■	■

Bibliography

Bibliography of relevant County Council Reports

Chichester—Preservation and Progress
  West Sussex County Council

Archaeological report
  Professor B. W. Cunliffe

Mini-bus feasiblity study
  West Sussex County Council

Bicycle Survey
  West Sussex County Council

Pedestrian Survey
  West Sussex County Council

Vehicular and pedestrian movement in the Chichester Study Area 1967
  West Sussex County Council

Coastal Report 1966
  West Sussex County Council

Copies of these reports are available from: The County Planning Officer, County Hall, Chichester, Sussex.

Acknowledgements

The authors wish to express appreciation to S. H. J. Roth, JP, AA Dipl, FRIBA, who made available fully detailed costings in respect of a number of notable old buildings he had acquired, renovated and brought into full use in a part of the city outside the Study Area.

Acknowledgement is also made for the help so willingly given by the members of the public, property owners and occupiers, youth clubs and school children; also to M. J. Cutten for the loan of his historical notes, and to Mrs J. Drewett for preparation of forms and Mrs C. Shippam for typing the manuscript.

Acknowledgement is made to the following for the use of photographs and reproductions:

Frontispiece C. Howard & Son Ltd
Fig. 2   Chichester Photographic Service Ltd
Fig. 3   Chichester Photographic Service Ltd
Fig. 5   C. Howard & Son Ltd
Fig. 8   Chichester Photographic Service Ltd
Fig. 9   The County Archivist
Fig. 11   The Director General, Ordnance Survey
Fig. 14   The Director General, Ordnance Survey
Fig. 40   Meridian Airmaps Ltd
Fig. 43   Chichester Photographic Service Ltd
Fig. 48   Meridian Airmaps Ltd
Fig. 49   The Curator, British Museum
Fig. 51   M. J. Cutten
Fig. 110   Chichester Photographic Service Ltd

Index

In order to assist in locating material, the index has been divided under nine main headings with sub-headings to each section. These are sub-divided further with references given to paragraph numbers, the main ones being in bold type.

The main headings are:

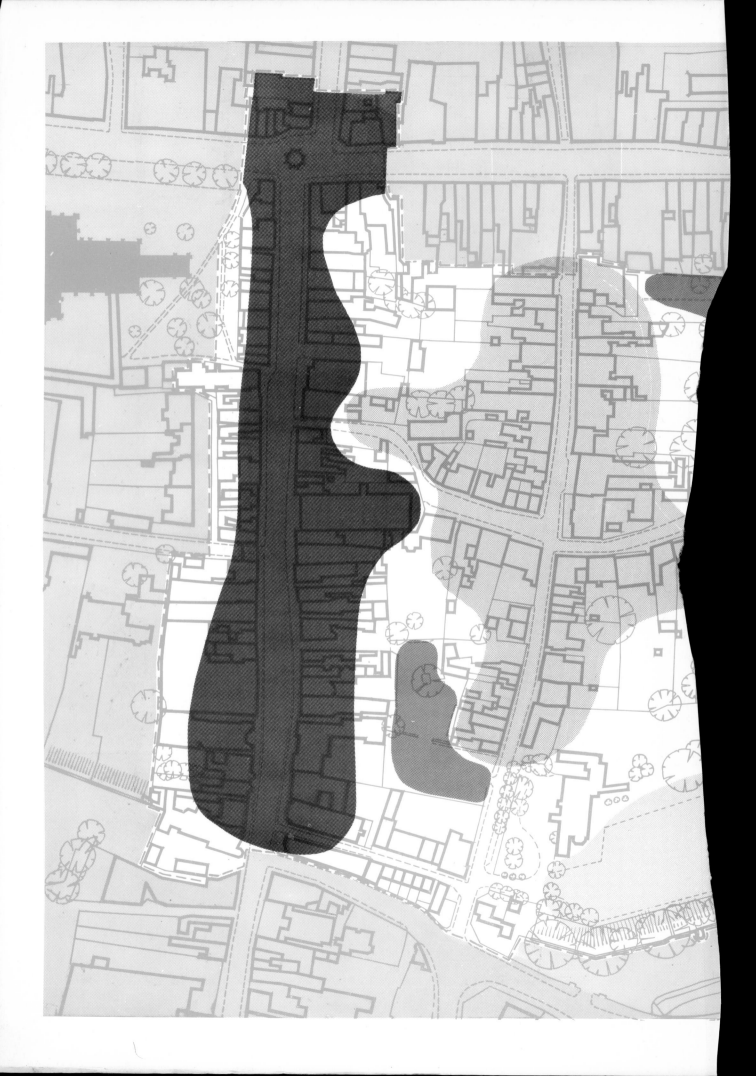

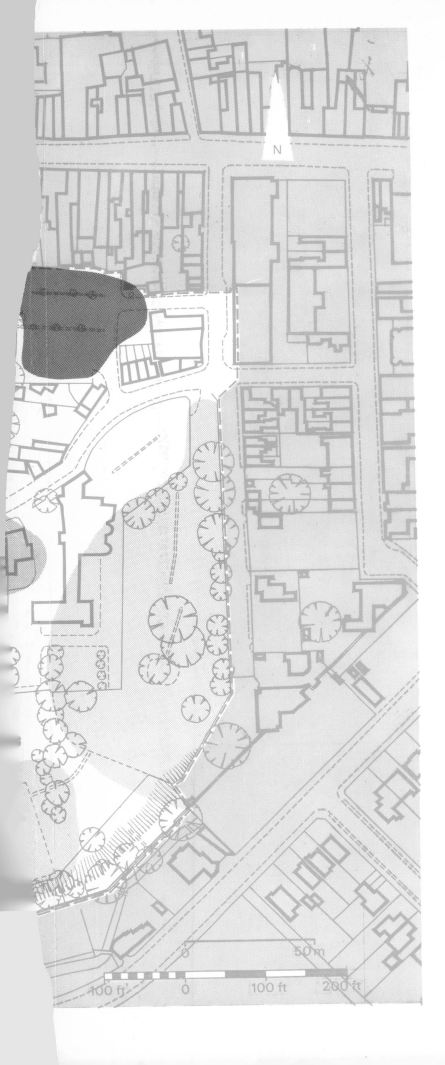

shopping streets

'Georgian' residential area

car parking/servicing

car parking

areas left unshaded have
no recognisable quality of
environment

N

50 m

100 ft   0   100 ft   200 ft

1

N

0   50 m

100 ft   0   100 ft   200 ft

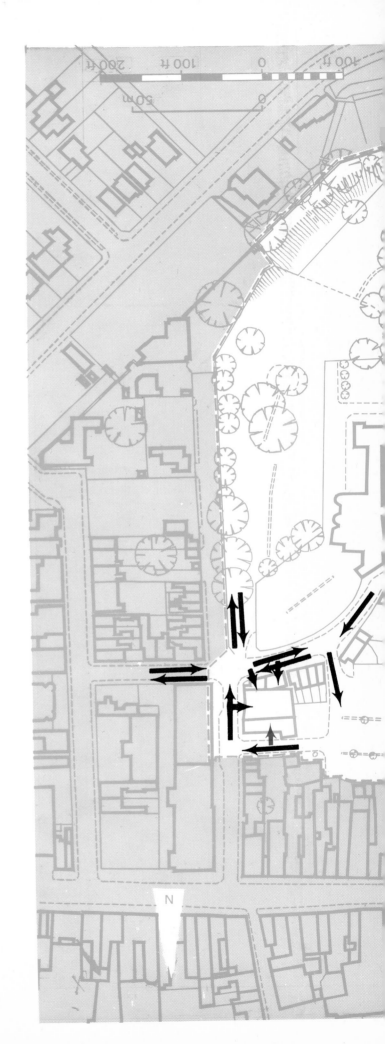

Key 3
Vehicular movements and servicing of properties — existing (6.79)

← direction of traffic flows

← shop servicing (heavy vehicles)

← office servicing (light vehicles)

3

Key 3   Vehicular movements and servicing of properties – existing (6.79)

amenity space/car parking

car parking/servicing

'Georgian residential area

shopping streets

traffic-free areas

Key 2
Environmental pattern — recommended
(7.03)

Key 4   Vehicular movements and servicing of properties – recommended (7.16)

4

Key 4
Vehicular movements and servicing of properties — recommended (7.16)

→ direction of traffic flows

pedestrian areas

➤ shop servicing (heavy vehicles)

➤ office servicing (light vehicles)

servicing space

○ turntable

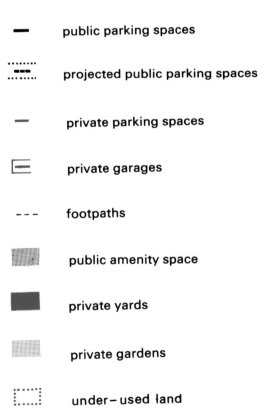

Key 5
Use and design of spaces — existing
(6.56)

▬	public parking spaces
┄┄	projected public parking spaces
▬	private parking spaces
⊟	private garages
- - -	footpaths
▦	public amenity space
■	private yards
▨	private gardens
⬚	under-used land
-	bicycle parking

N

0   50 m

100 ft   0   100 ft   200 ft

N

0   50 m

100 ft   0   100 ft   200 ft

—   private parking spaces in office hours
public parking spaces at other times

—   public parking spaces

—   private parking spaces

⊨   private garages

----   footpaths

    public amenity open space

    private yards

    private gardens

-     bicycle parking

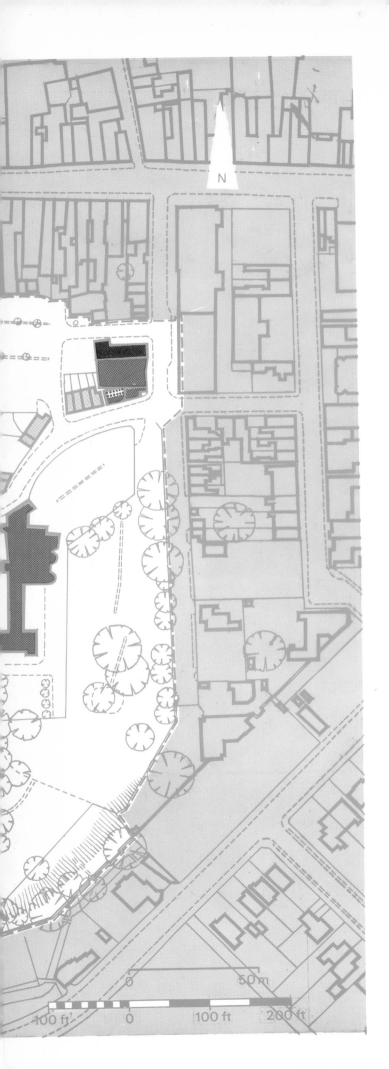

occupied space (proportional)

shopping

business

residential

garaging/storage

place of assembly

unoccupied space (proportional)

shopping

business

residential

areas of hatching above
are proportional to total
floor area
position of hatching indicates
floors involved
front of building = ground floor
back of building = top floor

N

0   50 m

100 ft   0   100 ft   200 ft

8

N

50 m

100 ft   0   100 ft   200 ft

Key 8
Uses of buildings — recommended
(7.66)

☐ uses unchanged

▨ shopping

▨ business

▨ residential

areas of hatching above
are proportional to total
floor area
position of hatching indicates
floors involved
front of building = ground floor
back of building = top floor

⌐⌐ demolition

⌐:⌐ new building

⌐ garaging

— boundary walls

Key 9   Storey heights and features of note – existing
(6.24)

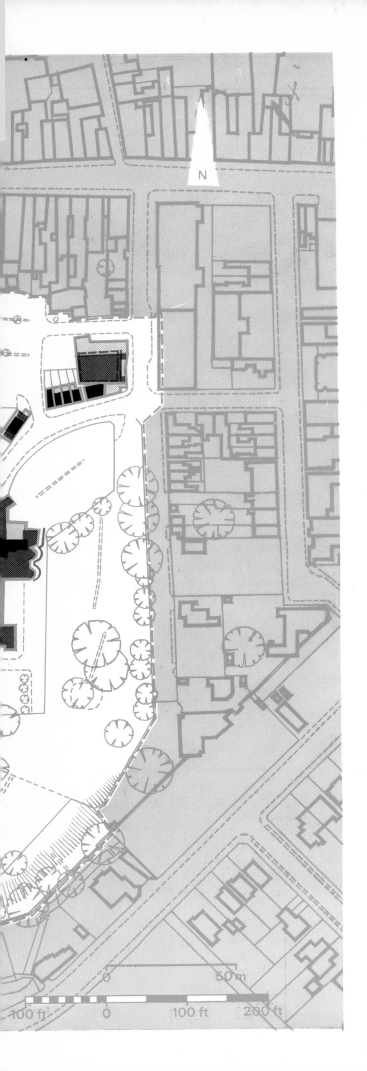

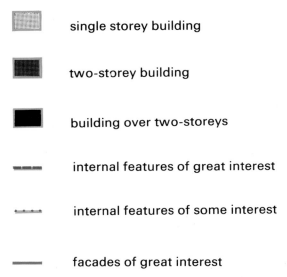

single storey building

two-storey building

building over two-storeys

internal features of great interest

internal features of some interest

facades of great interest

Key 10   **Age of buildings – existing** (6.24)
Restorations and alterations – recommended
(7.94)

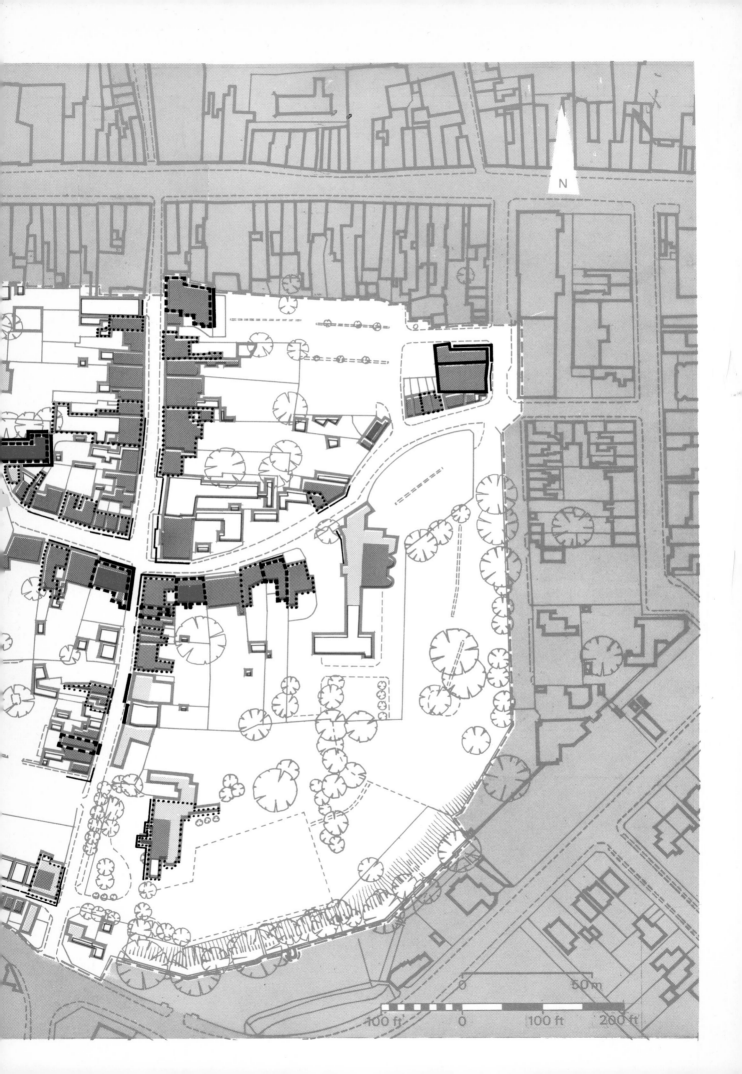

N

100 ft   0   100 ft   200 ft

0   50 m

Key 10 Age of buildings — existing (6.24)
**Restorations and alterations —
recommended** (7.94)

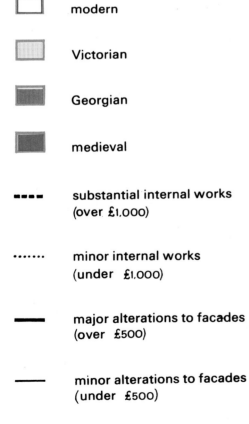

modern

Victorian

Georgian

medieval

---- substantial internal works
(over £1,000)

······· minor internal works
(under £1,000)

—— major alterations to facades
(over £500)

—— minor alterations to facades
(under £500)

Key 11   Listing of buildings – existing (6.24)

grade I

grade II

grade III

important street lines

N

0   50 m

100 ft   0   100 ft   200 ft

Key 12
Listing of buildings — recommended
(7.130)

existing

grade I

grade II

grade III

recommended

——— grade I

– – – grade IIa

---- grade IIb

······ grade III

Key 13   Synopsis of recommendations (7.162)

13

N

P
P
P
P
P
P
P
P
P
P
P
P
P
P

0   50 m

100 ft   0   100 ft   200 ft

Key 13
Synopsis of recommendations (7.162)

→ traffic flows

service areas

P car parks

traffic-free areas

amenity space

new buildings

new uses

---- demolished walls